A Practical Handbook for Building the Play Therapy Relationship

A Practical Handbook for Building the Play Therapy Relationship

MARIA GIORDANO, GARRY LANDRETH,
AND LESLIE JONES

JASON ARONSON

Lanham • Boulder • New York • Toronto • Oxford

Published in the United States of America
by Jason Aronson
An imprint of Rowman & Littlefield Publishers, Inc.

A wholly owned subsidary of
The Rowman & Littlefield Publishing Group, Inc.
4501 Forbes Boulevard, Suite 200, Lanham, Maryland 20706
www.rowmanlittlefield.com

PO Box 317
Oxford
OX2 9RU, UK

British Library Cataloguing in Publication Information Available

Library of Congress Cataloging-in-Publication Data

Giordano, Maria, 1964-
  A practical handbook for building the play therapy relationship / Maria Giordano, Garry Landreth,
and Leslie Jones.
      p. ; cm.
  Includes bibliographical references.
  ISBN 0-7657-0111-1 (pbk. : alk. paper)
  1. Play therapy—Handbooks, manuals, etc. I. Landreth, Garry L. II. Jones, Leslie, 1970- . III.
Title.
  [DNLM: 1. Play Therapy—methods. 2. Professional-Patient Relations. WM 450.5.P7 G497p
2005]
  RJ505.P6G54 2005
    615.8'5153—dc22   2004025857

Printed in the United States of America

™
The paper used in this publication meets the minimum requirements of American
National Standard for Information Sciences—Permanence of Paper for Printed Library
Materials, ANSI/NISO Z39.48-1992.

CONTENTS

INTRODUCTION

This resource guide is designed for practitioners, students, and play therapy supervisors who want a practical approach for learning or teaching the fundamental skills of building a therapeutic relationship in play therapy. Each skill is clearly defined and examples and rationale for using the skills are provided. Practice sections, discussion questions, and video session self-assessment questions provide additional opportunities to integrate the skills.

This guide can be used in supervised practicum and laboratory experiences in child and play therapy courses in counseling psychology, social work, counselor education and psychiatric nursing, and for intensive training workshops. The material and structure of this workbook provides valuable companion material to be used in conjunction with *Play Therapy: The Art of the Relationship* (second edition 2002) by Garry Landreth.

The philosophy and skills presented provide a foundation for play therapists who believe the therapeutic relationship is essential for the child's growth and development. Although six basic therapeutic responses are highlighted, the play therapist needs to integrate these responses into a personal style that communicates warmth, genuineness, and accurate empathic understanding of children's feelings, concerns, and experiences. Through working collaboratively with children and creating a supportive and safe environment, children feel freer to explore feelings, attitudes, and experiences that lead to personal understanding, change, and healing.

Developmentally, children are unable to understand and express their feelings, concerns, and experiences in the same way as adults. Play therapy provides a modality for children to communicate feelings and experiences they are not able to articulate. Children utilize play to express feelings, needs, and desires and use toys to express a wide range of feelings. Children also use toys to create scenarios which express needs such as nurturance, power, and control. The following are examples of how children express feelings, concerns, and experiences through play.

Example #1:

A child whose parents recently divorced used a doll family to act out a scene in which the parents remarried.

Example #2:

A child hid in the closet during a tornado and watched the news coverage of the impact of the tornado hours later. The child spent two play therapy sessions preparing for the tornado, hiding and expressing relief once the tornado had passed.

Example #3:

A four-year-old child shared a bed with a younger sibling the night the baby died of SIDS. The four-year-old came into the play room, grabbed the baby doll, sat on it and said "I killed it." This child continued to express anger and sadness in the following sessions.

Children use toys and art materials to express themselves and to create images and metaphors in their play. Sometimes a child will have the play therapist play a role the child usually experiences. The play therapist can gain a deeper understanding of the child's world by experiencing that world as represented by the child.

Example:

A child begins to scream and yell at the play therapist saying: "Son, I'm sick and tired of you being such a slob. If you don't clean up these toys right now, I'm throwing them all in the garbage, and you will never see them again." The child has provided the play therapist an opportunity to experience the intensity of his feelings of powerlessness, and the play therapist gains a deeper understanding of the child's world.

This resource was developed to provide information about the underlying principles and fundamental skills of play therapy. Definitions, examples and practice exercises, and discussion questions provide opportunities to integrate these skills and develop a deeper understanding of the play therapist's role in the therapeutic relationship.

CHAPTER 1

CHILD-CENTERED PLAY THERAPY

Child-centered play therapists believe in the importance of the therapeutic relationship and focus on the child with whom they are working — not the child's problem. Virginia Axline (1947) developed child-centered play therapy based upon the theoretical principles of Carl Roger's (1942) nondirective therapy. Axline described the play therapist as sensitive, accepting, and as having constant and deep appreciation for what the child is communicating verbally and non-verbally.

Child-centered play therapists believe that children have an innate drive toward independence and self-direction and children need permissiveness and acceptance to be themselves. This permissiveness and acceptance comes from significant people in the children's life. By experiencing a therapeutic relationship in which they feel valued and accepted, children learn to accept and value themselves (Axline, 1947).

Landreth (2002) described six objectives that assist the play therapist in developing a positive therapeutic relationship.

These objectives include:

- Establishing a safe atmosphere
- Understanding and accepting the child's world
- Encouraging expression of the child's emotional world
- Establishing a feeling of permissiveness
- Facilitating decision-making by the child
- Providing the child an opportunity to develop self-responsibility and self-control

BASIC PRINCIPLES OF PLAY SESSIONS

1. The child should be completely free to determine how he will use the time. The child leads and the therapist follows without making suggestions or asking questions.

2. The therapist's major task is to empathize with the child, and to understand the intent of the child's actions, thoughts, and feelings.

How does empathizing with the child impact the therapeutic relationship?

_____

_____

_____

_____

3. The therapist's next task is to communicate understanding to the child by appropriate comments, particularly, whenever possible, by verbalizing the feelings that the child is actively experiencing.

When you were a child, how did adults help you feel safe and understood?

_____

_____

_____

_____

4. The therapist is to be clear and firm about the few "limits" that are placed on the child.

GOALS OF THE PLAY THERAPY SESSIONS

1. To allow children, through the medium of play, to communicate thoughts, needs, and feelings.

2. To help children develop a more positive self-concept and more positive feelings of self-acceptance, self-respect, self-worth, and confidence.

3. To help children develop more self-direction, self-reliance, self-responsibility, and self-control.

4. To assist children in learning to identify and express feelings.

5. To help children develop an internal source of evaluation and to become more trusting of self.

Personal Reflection: Discuss your ideas about how play therapy may impact a child's life.

_____

_____

_____

_____

_____

_____

_____

This resource guide explains different types of therapeutic responses that can be used during play therapy sessions. When the therapist understands the rationale for specific responses, the therapist can discern when and how to use a response.

Although words carry powerful messages, the attitude in which the words are communicated is equally important. Responses made in an interactive and conversational manner sound natural and genuine. The therapist's body posture, facial expressions, and tone of voice convey interest, warmth, and acceptance of the child.

Understanding the rationale and wording of therapeutic responses will not produce a healing atmosphere. Instead, a genuine, trusting, empathic relationship is the foundation from which "the words" can empower and heal.

Personal Reflection: Discuss your ideas about how play therapy helps empower children.

_____

_____

_____

_____

_____

_____

_____

_____

_____

_____

_____

BASIC GUIDELINES FOR PLAY THERAPY

DON'T:

- Don't criticize any behavior.

- Don't praise the child.

- Don't ask leading questions.

- Don't allow interruptions of the session.

- Don't give information or teach.

- Don't initiate new behavior.

- Don't be passive or quiet.

Taken from: *Play Therapy: A Training Manual for Parents* by Louise Guerney (1972).

Personal Reflection: Discuss two of the guidelines and your thoughts about why it would be important to avoid these specific behaviors.

_____

_____

_____

_____

_____

_____

_____

DO:

- Do let the child lead.
- Do salute the child's power and encourage effort.
- Do join in the play as a follower.
- Do be verbally active.

Personal Reflection: Discuss the benefits of letting the child lead the therapeutic process.

_____

_____

_____

_____

_____

_____

_____

_____

_____

_____

_____

_____

_____

The play therapist's responses *should* convey:

1. "You are not alone; I am here with you."
2. "I hear/see you."
3. "I understand."
4. "I care."

Personal Reflection: Recall an adult in your childhood who conveyed one or more of the messages listed above. Briefly describe the significance of this relationship in your life.

_____

_____

_____

_____

_____

_____

_____

_____

_____

_____

_____

The play therapist's responses should *not* convey:

1. "I will solve your problems for you."
2. "I am responsible for making you happy."
3. "Because I understand you, that means I automatically agree with you."

Personal Reflection: Discuss two of the previous statements that the play therapist should avoid. How might a play therapist communicate these messages to the child?

_____

_____

_____

_____

_____

_____

_____

_____

_____

_____

CHAPTER 2

PLAY THERAPY ROOM AND TOYS

Play Therapy Room Location

Choose a location where the children will be least likely to disturb other clients or staff members.

Play Therapy Room Size (12 feet by 15 feet)

The room needs to be large enough that the child can comfortably move about and small enough that the play therapist can be present with the child without continually following the child around the room.

A room that is 150 to 200 square feet provides enough space for three children during group play therapy. More than three children in a room this size is not recommended. During the group process, children sometimes need time to regroup psychologically and to play alone without physical disturbance.

Play Therapy Room Characteristics

Flooring: Choose flooring that is durable and easy to clean such as vinyl tile squares. Avoid carpeting, which is difficult to keep clean. If the only space you have is carpeted, consider covering the carpet near the sandbox and the easel with a large piece of sheet vinyl.

Walls: Paint the walls with a product that is off-white, durable, and washable. Avoid colors that are dark, vibrant, or somber.

Sink: A sink with cold running water is recommended. Turn off the hot water valve under the sink and turn the cold water valve only half open so that the children can turn on the water full force without splashing water all over the room.

Shelving: Two of the walls will need shelves to provide space for toys and materials. Shelves need to be sturdy and fastened to the wall to ensure the children's safety. The top shelf should not exceed thirty-eight inches so that small children will be able to reach toys without assistance.

(Landreth, 2002)

Toys and Materials

- Children use toys to express thoughts, feelings, and experiences. The toys provided in the playroom are chosen to help children metaphorically or literally express themselves.

- Although the playroom is filled with toys, children who need play therapy are not engaging in carefree play. They are working hard and expressing feelings and concerns they find confusing and overwhelming.

- The play therapist is assisting the child in identifying and expressing feelings and in developing self-esteem, self-responsibility, and self-control. Different types of toys are chosen to help children express a variety of feelings and concerns.

The following is a basic list of toys that a child may use to communicate experiences, feelings, and needs. Although the toys are divided into categories, a child may be able to use a toy to express a need in more than one category.

Nurturing Toys

Baby doll, bottle, pacifier, brush, doll bed

Medical kit, bandages, white mask, medical shirt/white dress shirt

Cooking utensils, plastic food, dishes, pots and pans, stove

_____

Competency Toys

Blocks, Tinkertoys, ring toss, bowling, basketball hoop

_____

Aggressive-Release Toys

Aggressive plastic animals (tiger, lion, alligator, snake), bop bag, plastic soldiers,

Play-Doh (to smash and crush), rubber knife, dart gun, handcuffs

_____

Real-Life Toys

Dollhouse, doll family, puppets — family, police officer, doctor, nurse, family of animals

Play money, cash register, cleaning items (broom, dustpan, rag, mop)

Transportation (cars, trucks, planes, boats, school bus, ambulance, fire truck, helicopter)

Fantasy/Dress Up

Hats: firefighter, police officer — hat and badge, sailor, crown

Clothing: tie, sports jacket, dress shoes, purse, jewelry, dress

Masks: Lone Ranger–type mask, eye patch, sunglasses

Creative Expression and Emotional Release

Sand, water, blocks, easel and paint, crayons, markers, glue, blunt scissors, tape, Popsicle sticks, pipe cleaners, Play-Doh

DESIGNING AND ORGANIZING THE PLAY THERAPY ROOM

General layout of the play therapy rooms at the University of North Texas.

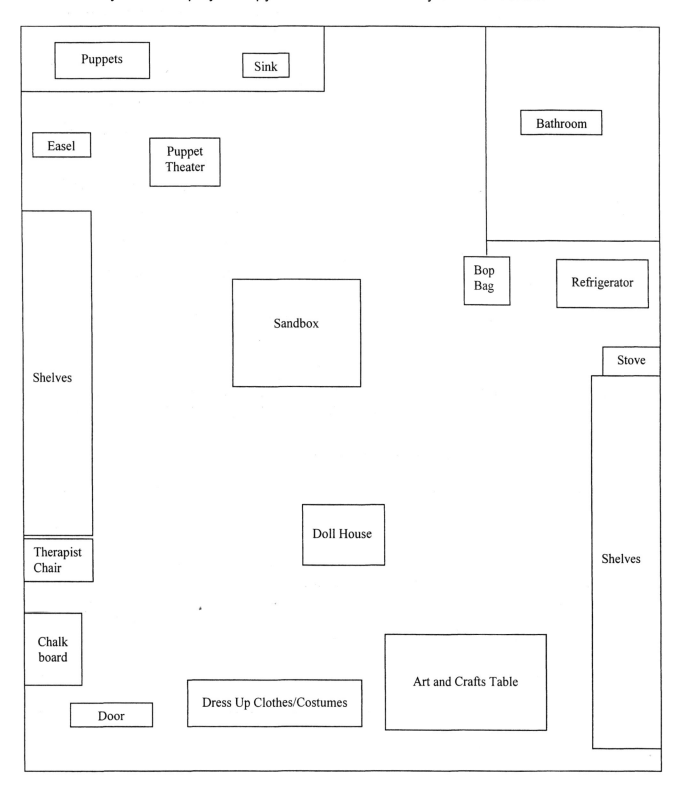

Toys need to be organized in a consistent manner so that children can return on a weekly basis and locate the toys in a familiar location.

How would you organize the toys listed below on the playroom shelves?

SHELF A

Top Shelf _____

_____

_____ — _____

Middle Shelf _____

_____

_____

Bottom Shelf _____

_____

Floor _____

_____

_____

Plane, Snakes, Ray Gun, Magnet, Boat, Rope, Cars, Polar Bear, Riding Toy, Dinosaurs, Machine Gun, Handcuffs/Key, Gorilla, Tinkertoys, Gumby, Zebra, Lions/Tigers, Cement Truck, Flashlight with Batteries, School Bus, Helicopter, Block Wagon, Front-End Loader, Farm Truck, Elephant, Dart Gun, Shark, Alligator, People, Crocodile, Cow, Dump Truck, Horse, Pig, Road Grader, Sheep, Knife, Tractor, Sword, Dog

How would you organize the toys listed below on the playroom shelves?

SHELF B

Top Shelf _____

_____

_____

Middle Shelf _____

_____

_____

Bottom Shelf _____

_____

_____

Floor _____

_____

_____

Crown, Baby Bed, Drum, Telephones (2), Martian Popping Toy, Barbie, Ken, Iron, Lone Ranger Mask, Blankets, Tambourine, Soft Football, Stuffed Toy, Extra Clothes for Barbie and Ken, Pacifier, Xylophone, Building Blocks, Firefighter Hat, Tissue, Doctor Kit (stethoscope, surgical mask, Band-Aids, blood pressure cuff, hypodermic needle, eye/ear light), Tube Noisemaker, Bowling Set, Dolls (diverse ethnicities), Kaleidoscope, Mallets, Etch A Sketch, Sailor Hat, Baby Bottles, Straw Hat, Pom-Pom, Magic Wand, Comb, Brush, Mirror, Plastic Ball, Wrestler, Nerf Ball, Cowboy or Cowgirl Hat, Art Paper, Egg Cartons, Cymbals

ORGANIZING THE PLAY THERAPY SHELVES

SHELF A

Top Shelf (Left to Right)

Sheep, Pig, Horse, Cow, Giraffe, Zebra, Elephant, Polar Bear, Gorilla,

Lions/Tigers, Shark, Alligator, Crocodile, Snakes, Dinosaurs

Middle Shelf (Left to Right)

(below domestic animals) School Bus, People, Dog, Plane, Gumby

(below aggressive animals) Machine Gun, Sword, Knife, Dart Gun, Ray Gun

Bottom Shelf (Left to Right)

(below school bus) Helicopter, Boat, Tractor, Cars

(below aggressive toys) Handcuffs/Key, Rope, Flashlight with Batteries, Tinkertoys, Magnet

Floor (Left to Right)

Road Grader, Block Wagon, Front-End Loader, Dump Truck, Cement Truck, Farm Truck, Riding Toy

Plane, Snakes, Ray Gun, Magnet, Boat, Rope, Cars, Polar Bear, Riding Toy, Dinosaurs, Machine Gun, Handcuffs/Key, Gorilla, Tinkertoys, Gumby, Zebra, Lions/Tigers, Cement Truck, Flashlight with Batteries, School Bus, Helicopter, Block Wagon, Front-End Loader, Farm Truck, Elephant, Dart Gun, Shark, Alligator, People, Crocodile, Cow, Dump Truck, Horse, Pig, Road Grader, Sheep, Knife, Tractor, Sword, Dog

SHELF B

Top Shelf (Left to Right)

Crown, Lone Ranger Mask, Magic Wand, Pom-Pom, Firefighter Hat, Sailor Hat, Straw Hat, Cowboy or Cowgirl Hat, Tissue

Middle Shelf (Left to Right)

Doctor Kit (open) (stethoscope, surgical mask, Band-Aids, blood pressure cuff, hypodermic needle, eye/ear light), Telephones (2), Iron, Pacifier, Baby Bottles (large, small, toy)

Drum, Cymbals, Tambourine, Kaleidoscope, Xylophone, Mallets, Tube Noisemaker, Etch A Sketch

Bottom Shelf (Left to Right)

Barbie, Ken (diverse ethnicities), Extra Clothing, Stuffed Toy, Comb, Brush, Mirror, Wrestler

Martian Popping Toy, Soft Football, Nerf Ball, Bowling Set, Plastic Ball, Art Paper, Egg Cartons (2)

Floor (Left to Right)

Baby Bed, Dolls (diverse ethnicities), Blankets, Building Blocks

Crown, Baby Bed, Drum, Telephones (2), Martian Popping Toy, Barbie, Ken, Iron, Lone Ranger Mask, Blankets, Tambourine, Soft Football, Stuffed Toy, Extra Clothes for Barbie and Ken, Pacifier, Xylophone, Building Blocks, Firefighter Hat, Tissue, Doctor Kit (stethoscope, surgical mask, Band-Aids, blood pressure cuff, hypodermic needle, eye/ear light), Tube Noisemaker, Bowling Set, Dolls (diverse ethnicities), Kaleidoscope, Mallets, Etch A Sketch, Sailor Hat, Baby Bottles, Straw Hat, Pom-Pom, Magic Wand, Comb, Brush, Mirror, Plastic Ball, Wrestler, Nerf Ball, Cowboy or Cowgirl Hat, Art Paper, Egg Cartons, Cymbals

ORGANIZING OTHER AREAS OF THE PLAY THERAPY ROOM

Art and Crafts Table

Watercolor Set, Finger Paint, Masking Tape, Scissors, Glue, Pen, Rubber Bands, Clear Tape, Markers, Crayons, Craft Sticks, Play-Doh, Cookie Cutters, Pizza Cutter, Paper, Stapler, Pipe Cleaners, Straws

Puppets

Alligator, Dog, Dragon, Lion, Bear, Wolf, Frog, Mouse, Police, Nurse, Doctor, Family (diverse ethnicities)

Costumes

Cape, Purse (2), Necklaces (2), Shirt, Dress, Tie, Shoes, Jacket

Dollhouse

Furniture–bathroom, living room, bedroom, kitchen
Family–five people (diverse ethnicities)

Easel

Paint–brown, red, green, yellow, blue, black, white
Easel brushes (7), Easel Paper and Two Clips, Paint Apron

Chalkboard

Chalk–white and multicolored
Eraser

Sandbox

Sifter, Spoon (large), Bucket, Scoop, Army Figures (outside box near corner of the sandbox)

Housekeeping And Kitchen Items

Refrigerator

Cereal Box, Cracker Box, Baking Powder/Soda, Processed Food, Ice Tray, Soda, Milk, Bread, Chicken, Meat, Eggs, Vegetables, Fruit

Stove

Pot (on top of stove), Frying Pan with Egg, Muffin Tin, Cake Pan, Pots (2)

Dish Rack

Plates, Bowls, Cups, Silverware, Funnel, Strainer, Mixer

CONCERNS RELATED TO TOYS USED TO EXPRESS AGGRESSION

The use of certain aggressive toys may not be tolerated in some school or clinic settings. This is usually because adults in this setting are concerned that playing out aggressive behavior with dart guns, rubber knives, and toy machine guns desensitizes children to violence. In a culture where violence is exonerated in movies and video games, there is concern that violent play reinforces the notion that violence is an appropriate means of expressing anger and aggression.

The Difference in the Playroom

1. Limits are set by the play therapist. "People aren't for hitting, hurting, shooting, etc."

2. Children learn to express anger using inanimate objects and ultimately learn to express anger using words.

3. Parents who bring children to play therapy because of aggressive behavior have reported a decrease in the children's aggressive behavior outside the playroom. The therapist helps the child identify feelings of anger and frustration. The child is also helped to express aggression in a manner that does not hurt himself, the therapist, the toys, or the playroom. The child ultimately learns to identify feelings of anger and aggression and to express them verbally. As a result, the therapeutic process helps the child express anger in a non-violent manner.

CHAPTER 3

PRIOR TO THE FIRST PLAY THERAPY SESSION

Prepare Administrative Forms for the Parent

1. Informed Consent

Have the parent sign two copies of the "Informed Consent" during the parent consult. Have the parent keep a copy for his records and place a copy in the client's file.

2. Professional Disclosure

Have the parent sign two copies of your "Professional Disclosure" during the parent consult. Have the parent keep a copy for his records and place a copy in the client's file.

3. Assessment Forms

Each parent, the teacher, and other significant adults in the child's life observe and experience different strengths and struggles of the child. Teachers have been surprised to learn that a child who follows instructions and gets along well with classmates is experiencing difficulty following parental guidelines at home. Children's behavior changes in different environments with different adults. Therefore, it is helpful to gain the parent(s) and teacher's perspective of the child's behavior.

4. Divorce Decree/Child Custody

If divorced, obtain a copy of the Divorce Decree/Child Custody Document (file). You will need to obtain the signature from the parent designated by the court as the "managing conservator."

Additional Information Needed for the First Parent Consultation

1. Brochure for the parent about play therapy (available through the Association for Play Therapy)
2. A Child's First Book about Play Therapy
3. Appointment Card for parent to give to the child

Goals of the First Parent Consultation

1. Develop a positive rapport/relationship with the parent.
2. Find out what made parent(s) seek help and what they are hoping to gain from bringing their child to play therapy.
3. Learn about the child.
4. Complete administrative forms.
5. Educate parent(s) about play therapy.

Personal Reflection: Describe how you would facilitate the first parent consultation so that you accomplish the five goals.

_____

_____

_____

_____

_____

_____

FIRST MEETING WITH THE PARENT/GUARDIAN

The following is an outline of discussion items designed to provide the play therapist with a greater understanding of the child, parent(s), and the family.

Main Concern What has been happening that made you decide to bring your child to play therapy? (First begin, frequency, time of day, where)

Attempted Solutions What types of things have you tried?

Changes What do you hope will happen as a result of bringing your child for counseling?

Relationships Relationship with each parent/caregiver (if divorced, visitation, what visits are like, relationship between parents)

Siblings / Teachers / Other Adults

Peers (plays with children own age, older, younger; leader, follower, loner)

Childhood Illnesses, Accidents, Life Stressors (loss—person, pet, divorce, change in schools, moves)

Counseling Has your child received prior counseling? (With whom, why started, duration, effectiveness) (If yes, have parent sign release form for records.)

Medication Is your child on medication?

School General attitude toward school; Parent's perception of teacher(s) and child's progress

Counseling	If parent is stressed and discusses many personal issues, offer individual counseling, parent consultation, or filial therapy.
Handouts	"What Parents and Children Need to Know" "A Child's First Book about Play Therapy"
Consistency	Discuss importance of consistency in bringing child for play therapy. Children feel more secure when they have structure and the ability to predict what is going to happen in life.

First Meeting

- Discuss how you will greet the child. Explain the importance of not talking about the child in front of the child. If the parent would like to discuss a concern or recent experience about his child, ask the parent to call you prior to the session. Advise the parent to make certain his child is not able to hear the phone conversation.

- Ask parents to take their children to the bathroom prior to the play therapy session.

- Meet with the parent on a regular basis (at least every other week). Talk with the parent about how the child is doing at home and at school. Provide general information about the child's growth. It is important to maintain a supportive and collaborative relationship with the child's parent. Parents often feel isolated from the therapeutic process due to the play therapist's concern about confidentiality.

- Maintain and honor confidentiality while involving the parent.

Confidentiality	Give examples of feedback you will be giving parent: (Child may want me to do everything for them; do you see this kind of behavior at home?)
Gifts	Discuss with parent issue of not receiving gifts.

Fees	Discuss fees and how you will collect fees at the end of each session.
Intake Forms	Have parent read and sign: Informed Consent and Professional Disclosure. Answer any questions about the content of these forms.
Complete Forms	Tell parents: "Assessment forms are important to give us a better understanding of your child. Please complete them and bring them with you before I see your child next week."
Show Playroom	Explain why therapists use play media (cognitive development; children don't articulate feelings and thoughts as do adults; use toys to deal with emotions and express concerns).

CHAPTER 4

STRUCTURING THE PLAY THERAPY SESSION

In the Waiting Room

1. Have the child use the bathroom prior to the play session.

2. When meeting the child in the waiting room state:

"We can go to the playroom now."

- Refrain from asking the child: "Do you want to go to the playroom now?"

- This question inaccurately implies that the child has a choice.

Opening the Session

"Alex, this is our playroom, and this is a place where you can play with the toys *in a lot of* the ways you'd like to."

- It would be untrue to say "you can play with the toys in *any* of the ways you would like to." There are limits in the playroom.

Personal Reflection: Briefly describe how you would introduce yourself to the child and the statement you would use to open the first play therapy session.

_____

_____

_____

_____

Closing the Session

1. "Alex, we have five more minutes in the playroom for today."

2. If Alex is very absorbed in his play, state:
   "Alex, we have one more minute left in the playroom for today."

3. "Alex, our time is up for today. It's time to go to the waiting room where your mother is." (Play therapist stands and walks toward the door.)

4. If the child does not want to leave the playroom, state:
   "Alex, I know you really like being here, but our time is up for today. You can come back again next week."

- It will take some children several minutes to leave the playroom. Repeat the closing statement several times if needed. Use a firmer voice each time, and slowly walk toward the door.

- Once you have stated "time is up for today," refrain from making responses that acknowledge behavior/tracking responses or other therapeutic responses that address the content of the play. This type of response focuses on the child's current behavior, encourages the child to continue playing, and does not reinforce the message that it is time for the child to leave the playroom.

CREATING A THERAPEUTIC ENVIRONMENT

1. Leaning Forward and Open Body Posture

The therapist wants to create a warm and accepting environment for the child. A therapist's non-verbal behavior impacts the child's perceptions of the therapist's approachability and openness. By leaning forward and having an open body posture, the therapist conveys concern and interest in the child's world.

2. Relaxed and Comfortable

A therapist who is relaxed and comfortable will seem calm and emotionally available. A child who ordinarily lives in a stressful environment may be more likely to approach a nurturing therapist who is calm and relaxed.

3. Appear Interested in the Child

Interest in the child can be communicated through non-verbal and verbal responses. The therapist's body posture, facial expressions, and accurate empathic responses indicate a genuine interest in the child's world.

Personal Reflection: Discuss your personal qualities and strengths that will help you create a therapeutic environment.

_____

_____

_____

_____

CONVEYING AN UNDERSTANDING OF
THE CHILD'S WORLD

- A therapist who is genuine and strives to understand the child's perspective conveys a desire to understand the "child's world."

- Accurate reflections will usually convey an understanding of the child's world. This understanding is also conveyed through creating a psychological climate of genuine caring and empathy.

- The therapist's general attitude and openness communicates the therapist is in tune with the child. A therapist who uses a receptive tone of voice and body language shows a desire to understand and make a connection with the child.

Personal Reflection: Describe in your own words how you will convey an understanding of your client's world/world view, feelings, and experiences.

_____

_____

_____

_____

_____

_____

_____

_____

FACILITATING CHILD'S UNDERSTANDING OF SELF

What is facilitating child's understanding of self?

The therapist assists the child in developing a greater self-awareness by making specific responses such as a reflection of feeling. Through increasing personal awareness of feelings, the child has a greater understanding of his emotional state. Also, responses that acknowledge the child's competencies help the child gain a clearer understanding of personal strengths and abilities.

Two Therapeutic Responses that Facilitate Understanding of Self

- **Reflecting Feelings**

Accurate feeling reflections help children create a deeper understanding of self. The child learns to identify and communicate his feelings to others.

Example: Sometimes you feel all alone.

List five examples of statements that reflect feelings.

1. _____

2. _____

3. _____

4. _____

5. _____

- **Esteem-Building Statements**

Esteem-building statements help children recognize competencies and gain a further understanding of their strengths.

Example: You figured out how to put those pieces together.

The child hears a message that he is capable of accomplishing this task independently. This type of response helps a child identify and acknowledge his positive qualities and abilities.

List five examples of statements that build self-esteem.

1. _____

2. _____

3. _____

4. _____

5. _____

These two therapeutic responses will be addressed in more detail in the following pages.

CHAPTER 5

ACKNOWLEDGING NON-VERBAL BEHAVIOR
(TRACKING BEHAVIOR)

What is acknowledging non-verbal behavior?

- The therapist responds to the child's actions and non-verbal play. The therapist states what the therapist sees and observes the child doing.

Examples

- You are pushing that (car) right through there (tunnel).
- You are putting lots of sand in that (bucket).
- You are kicking that (bop bag).

    Note: The therapist does not identify the item until the child does.

Why acknowledge non-verbal behavior?

- When children provide little to no verbal content to respond to and are not expressing any particular emotion, acknowledging children's behavior helps children feel you are interested in their world, you care about their world, and you are striving to understand their world.

Rationale for Not Labeling Toys

- When play therapists label toys and behaviors according to an adult perspective, inaccurate assumptions and responses may be made.

Example: If a child is pushing a block into the sand and the therapist responds by stating "You are pushing that block deep into the sand." The child could be pretending that the block is a bulldozer, a spaceship, or an animal.

Response that avoids labeling: "You're pushing that into the sand."

- When a play therapist inaccurately labels a toy, some children will correct the therapist and some will not. Children may feel less understood by a play therapist if the toy is inaccurately labeled.

- Not labeling toys creates a more permissive environment that encourages the children to be creative. Children may feel freer to use toys in other ways than in a conventional manner. Use non-descriptive words such as "them, that, those, there."

Acknowledging Non-Verbal Behavior — Appropriate Amount of Responses

1. Responding Infrequently

If the therapist is silent during the child's play, the child will begin to feel watched or that the therapist is uninterested in the child. Instead, the therapist wants the child to feel as though the therapist is a part of the play.

This is similar to being in a conversation with an adult. Adults know that a person cares and hears them when the person listens and verbally responds. In like manner, the play therapist listens with ears and eyes and verbalizes what she hears and sees.

2. Responding Too Frequently

If the therapist acknowledges non-verbal behavior too frequently, the therapist may sound like a sports commentator providing a play-by-play action.

This type of commentary does not sound genuine and conversational. The child may experience the comments as intrusive. The responses need to be stated in a genuine and conversational manner.

Acknowledging Non-Verbal Behavior — Personalizing the Response

Begin the response with **"You're" or "you are."** This personalizes the message and places the focus on the child instead of the toy. It also promotes a feeling of the child being in control.

EXAMPLE:

The child is playing with a car, which he has previously identified as a car, and is driving it around in large circles.

Focus is on the child. (Helps the child feel empowered.)

- *You're* driving that car around and around.

Focus is on the toy. (Depersonalized message; does not help child feel important or empowered.)

- *That car* is going around and around.

- During the first play therapy session, the therapist may be more talkative and acknowledge non-verbal behavior more frequently to help alleviate the child's anxiety.

- If the child is very absorbed in play, fewer responses may be needed.

Discussion Question: What does the child experience when the play therapist genuinely and effectively acknowledges non-verbal behavior? How does the child then feel?

PRACTICE ACKNOWLEDGING NON-VERBAL BEHAVIOR

1. The child builds a tall tower using building blocks and knocks them over.

Response: You're _____

2. The child brushes the baby doll's hair.

Response: _____

3. The child wipes off the shelves and reorganizes the toys.

Response: _____

4. The child puts on the firefighter's hat, takes it off, and puts on the police officer's helmet. The child takes off that hat and puts on a crown.

Response: _____

5. The child silently paints a scene of a house, a sun, and a tree. Then, he covers the scene with black paint.

Response: _____

6. The child takes the stethoscope out of the medical kit and listens to her heart.

Response: _____

7. The child opens the cash register and silently counts the money. He returns the money to the cash register drawer and closes the drawer.

Response: _____

Video Review and Reflection:

Review a video of your play therapy session. Listen for responses that acknowledge non-verbal behavior. Would you increase or decrease the number of these responses during specific parts of the session?

Do your responses seem genuine and sound conversational?

If you need to increase the responses, select eight opportunities you missed to make a response that acknowledges non-verbal behavior.

Describe the play behavior and write the response.

What questions do you have about using this skill?

EXAMPLE OF INEFFECTIVE AND EFFECTIVE ACKNOWLEDGMENT OF NON-VERBAL BEHAVIOR

General Information

A four-year-old boy was brought to play therapy by his mother due to separation anxiety. The mother reported that her son cried whenever she left the room at home and was only consoled by her. She further stated that he was quiet around new people and often had difficulty warming up to even family members. She also reported that he had always been close to her and was not very excited about the idea of having a new baby brother or sister in a few months.

Excerpt from a Play Session

Acknowledgment of Non-Verbal Behavior

Child:

(Enters the room and begins to look around at all the toys without talking and an anxious look on his face.)

Therapist:

What would you like to play with today?

Commentary:

The therapist begins this session by asking a question and taking the lead from the child. The therapist is assuming that the child does want to play and is sending the child a message that the therapist expects the child to play with the toys in the room. Instead, the therapist wants to send the message that whatever the child decides to do is acceptable during the playtime. The therapist wants to allow the child to lead the direction of the playtime instead of taking control of the activities.

Additionally, the therapist failed to respond to the child's feelings. By responding to the child's feelings and non-verbal behavior, the therapist sends the message that they are fully present with the child and will allow the child to express their feelings and thoughts during the playtime.

Corrected Response

Child:	(Enters the room and begins to look around at all the toys without talking and an anxious look on his face.)
Therapist:	You're not quite sure about being here and you are checking out all the things in this room.
Commentary:	An inactive child may be difficult for a beginning play therapist because they assume all children will want to play in the playroom. By responding to the behavior and actions that are observed the therapist lets the child know that they are present and focused on him.

CASE STUDY PRACTICE

Write a therapist response to acknowledge the child's non-verbal behavior.

After you have written a response to each situation, turn to the next page and compare your responses with recommended play therapist responses. Resist the urge to look at the recommended responses before you write your own.

Child: (Pushes a truck across the sandbox.) Vrrmm.

Therapist: _____

Child: (Scoops the sand and puts it in the back of the truck.)

Therapist: _____

Child: (Pushes the truck back to the other side of the sandbox; dumps out the sand.)

Therapist: _____

Child: (Gets up and begins looking around the room.)

Therapist: _____

Child: (Picks up the airplane and drops it in the sandbox, and begins looking for more toys to use in the sandbox.)

Therapist: _____

Child: (Puts the plastic soldiers in the sandbox and begins to set up a scene using all the toys he has brought over.)

Therapist: _____

Child: (Puts the plastic soldiers in a straight line, then begins to build a wall around them.)

Therapist: _____

Child: (Takes the truck and plane out of the sandbox.)

Therapist: _____

Child: (Begins to enact a battle with the plastic soldiers.) Pow, bang, boom.

Therapist: _____

Child: (Knocks over several of the plastic soldiers then covers them with sand.)

Therapist: _____

EXAMPLE: THERAPIST RESPONSES FOR ACKNOWLEDGING NON-VERBAL BEHAVIOR

Child: (Pushes a truck across the sandbox.) Vrrmm.

Therapist: You're pushing that right across there.

Child: (Scoops the sand and puts it in the back of the truck.)

Therapist: Pouring that right in there.

Child: (Pushes the truck back to the other side of the sandbox; dumps out the sand.)

Therapist: Now back over there and dumping it right there.

Child: (Gets up and begins looking around the room.)

Therapist: Looking around for something else.

Child: (Picks up the airplane and drops it in the sandbox, and begins looking for more toys to use in the sandbox.)

Therapist: Putting that right there and seeing what else you want to use.

Child: (Puts the plastic soldiers in the sandbox and begins to set up a scene using all the toys he has brought over.)

Therapist: You've got all you want for now and you are getting them the way you want them.

Child: (Puts the plastic soldiers in a straight line, then begins to build a wall around them.)

Therapist: You're lining them up and making a wall to protect them.

Child: (Begins to enact a battle with the plastic soldiers.) Pow, bang, boom.

Therapist: Sounds like they are really fighting.

Child: (Knocks over several of the plastic soldiers then covers them with sand.)

Therapist: Looks like those got hit and now you are covering them up.

CHAPTER 6

REFLECTING CONTENT

What is reflecting content?

- The therapist repeats in slightly different words something that the child has said.

Examples

- The child is working in the sandbox and states "There is going to be a big earthquake soon. No one can keep it from happening; not even Superman."

  Response: No one can help stop the earthquake.

- The child placed the dishes on the floor and stated:
  "It's time for dinner, everyone come to dinner this very minute."

  Response: You're letting everyone know that dinner is ready to eat.

Why reflect content?

- Reflecting content helps the child know that you hear and understand the content of her message. It also provides the child with the opportunity to hear the message so that she can hear what she has said. This helps validate her perspective and clarify her understanding of self.

- When presented with a choice to reflect feeling or content, respond to the child's feeling or combine a feeling and content response. If a child's feelings are not obvious, listen to the tone of voice the child uses to help discern the feeling within the message.

PRACTICE REFLECTING CONTENT

- Although other responses may be more appropriate, practice making content reflections.

    1. The child is playing with the doll and states: "She's hungry; so I'm going to feed her."

Response: _____

    2. The child is playing with the soldiers and states: "He's going to kill all the bad guys."

Response: _____

    3. The child is playing with the doll family and states: "It's time for everyone to go to sleep."

Response: _____

    4. The child is sorting out the money and states: "I'm going to buy everything in this room."

Response: _____

    5. The child is playing with the puppets. One puppet says to the other puppet: "I'm going to have a birthday party tomorrow."

Response: _____

Discussion Question: What does the child learn when the play therapist responds to the content of the child's message? How does the child then feel?

Video Review and Reflection: Video a play therapy session you have with a child. Review the video and listen for responses that reflect content. Identify eight times when you were silent and could have reflected content. Write down responses you could have made or content responses you would like to improve.

Video Review Response Format:

Child: What the child said.

Therapist: Your response or note that no response was made.

Corrected Response: What you wish you had said.

Reason for Corrected Response: Explain why the corrected response is more effective and/or how it impacts the child.

EXAMPLE OF INEFFECTIVE AND EFFECTIVE REFLECTION OF CONTENT

General Information

Tyler's mother, Angie, brought seven-year-old Tyler in for play therapy because he is having difficulty accepting her relationship with his stepfather, Alan. Tyler's biological father left the family when Tyler was eighteen months old and Tyler has not had contact with him since that time. Tyler and his mother spent a lot of time together in the evenings and weekends prior to meeting Alan. When Angie met Alan two years ago, Tyler became very angry when they began dating. Angie explained that she thought Tyler would come to accept Alan but Tyler has only become more verbal in his hatred for Alan.

Excerpt from the First Play Therapy Session with Tyler

Reflection of Content

Child: Tyler looked at the bop bag and then put sand in the plastic cup and said "I'm going poison his orange juice and then he will die."

Therapist: "You decided to put sand into the plastic cup."

Commentary: The therapist missed an opportunity to respond to the significance of Tyler's communication. The content of Tyler's communication was more significant than the fact that he was putting sand into the cup. Acknowledging non-verbal behavior is an important response to use when a child is not communicating verbally. It lets the child know that you are present and care about him or her.

Corrected Response

Child: Tyler looked at the bop bag and then put sand in the plastic cup and said "I'm going poison his orange juice and then he will die."

Therapist: "You want the poisonous orange juice to kill him."

Commentary: Tyler's comment may surprise some beginning play therapists who may find it difficult to acknowledge his statement. Avoiding the statement may communicate to Tyler that there is something "wrong" about his metaphorical play.

CASE STUDY PRACTICE

Write a therapist response for reflecting the child's content.

After you have written a response to each situation, turn to the next page and compare your responses with recommended play therapist responses. Resist the urge to look at the recommended responses before you write your own.

Child: Hey, who was in here? (Child bends down and is looking into the sandbox and points at footprints in the sand.)

Therapist: _____

Child: Who did it? Let me see the bottom of your shoe.

Therapist: _____

Child: Naah. (No.)

Therapist: _____

Child: (Begins covering the footprints with the shovel. Joshua puts his hand in the sand and begins to move the sand from one side of the sandbox to the other.) Earthquake!

Therapist: _____

Child: Batman and Robin are here! (Joshua drops sand on the earthquake.)

Therapist: _____

Child: But they (Batman and Robin) can't stop it.

Therapist: _____

Child: This can!

Therapist: _____

Child: (Joshua begins burying his left hand.) Batman is dead. (Voice tone
             sounds sad.)

Therapist: _____

Child: No, Superman is burying him.

Therapist: _____

Child: Here comes a nice army tank. He can stop the earthquake. He let
             Batman out. I'm free! (Sounds happy.)

Therapist: _____

Child: The walls are coming in again. I'm scared.

Therapist: _____

Child: He fell in and he's trapped. (Points at hand previously labeled the
             bad guy.)

Therapist: _____

Child: Now, stay away!

Therapist: _____

Child: (Looks at hands.) Mean guy and good guy.

Therapist: _____

EXAMPLE: THERAPIST RESPONSES FOR REFLECTING CONTENT

Child: Hey, who was in here? (Child bends down and is looking into the sandbox and points at footprints in the sand.)

Therapist: You noticed that there are footprints in there.

Child: Who did it? Let me see the bottom of your shoe.

Therapist: You want to see the bottom of my shoe and see if it's like that shoe.

Child: Naah.

Therapist: No, you don't think so.

Child: (Begins covering the footprints with the shovel. Joshua puts his hand in the sand and begins to move the sand from one side of the sandbox to the other.) Earthquake!

Therapist: Here comes an earthquake.

Child: Batman and Robin are here! (Joshua drops sand on the earthquake.)

Therapist: Batman and Robin dropped some things on the earthquake.

Child: But they can't stop it.

Therapist: No matter what they do; it's not enough to stop that earthquake.

Child: This can!

Therapist: Oh, that can stop it.

Child: (Joshua begins burying his left hand.) Batman is dead. (Voice tone sounds sad.)

Therapist: You are sad. Batman has died and you're burying him.

Child: No, Superman is burying him.

Therapist: Oh, Superman is burying Batman.

Child: Here comes a nice army tank. He can stop the earthquake. He let Batman out. I'm free! (Sounds happy.)

Therapist: Batman is so happy to be free again.

Child: The walls are coming in again. I'm scared.

Therapist: He's so scared; he doesn't know what to do.

Child: He fell in and he's trapped. (Points at hand previously labeled the bad guy.)

Therapist: Oh, the bad guy fell in the trap.

Child: Now, stay away!

Therapist: You warned him to stay away.

Child: (Looks at hands.) Mean guy and good guy.

Therapist: Some guys are mean and some are good.

CHAPTER 7

REFLECTING FEELINGS

Why reflect feelings?

- Reflecting feelings communicates understanding and acceptance of children's feelings and needs. It also shows children that you are interested and that you want to understand them.

- This process helps children understand, accept, and label their feelings.

- Children also learn how to verbally communicate their feelings. If a feeling is expressed and goes unrecognized, children may think that the feeling or expression is not acceptable.

RECOGNIZING FEELINGS

You seem frustrated that . . .   You look excited.

You look happy . . .   You are sad.

You're angry that . . .   You really like . . .

You're confused . . .   You don't like . . .

Write twenty words that describe "feelings" (i.e., happy, sad, afraid).

_____

_____

_____

_____

_____

FEELING WORDS

Aggravated	Angry	Annoyed	Irritated
Confused	Surprised	Embarrassed	Frustrated
Scared	Afraid	Frightened	Nervous
Exhausted	Overwhelmed	Shocked	Worried
Sad	Lonely	Unhappy	Unloved
Happy	Content	Excited	Pleased
Strong	Confident	Proud	Satisfied
Competent	Determined	Secure	Strong
Loving	Appreciative	Caring	Enthusiastic
Playful	Carefree	Relieved	

PRACTICE: REFLECTING FEELINGS

1. You state, "*Terry*, this is our very special room. You can do a lot of things you want to do in this playroom." The child is smiling, jumping up and down, and states "Really?!"

Response: _____.

2. The child is playing with the dollhouse family. One doll is yelling at the other doll.

Response: _____.

3. The child is pretending to set the dinner table. The child smiles and states, "I know just where everything goes."

Response: _____.

4. The child hits the bop bag and smiles.

Response: _____.

5. The child puts the handcuffs on you and laughs.

Response: _____.

6. The child drops the water, and it splashes all over the floor.

Response: _____.

7. The child aims the dart gun at the ceiling light. You set a limit and the child throws the gun down on the floor and stamps his/her feet.

Response: _____.

8. The child carefully and tentatively opens the medical kit. The child begins to take out the syringe, and quickly drops it back into the kit and begins playing with a different toy.

Response: _____.

Video Review and Reflection: Video a play therapy session you have with a child. Review the video and listen for responses that reflect feeling. Identify eight times when you were silent and could have reflected feeling. Write responses using this format.

Video Review Response Format:

Child: What the child said or did.

Therapist: Your response or note that no response was made.

Corrected Response: What you wish you had said.

Reason for Corrected Response: Explain why the corrected response is more effective and/or how it impacts the child.

EXAMPLE OF INEFFECTIVE AND EFFECTIVE REFLECTION OF FEELING

General Information

A seven-year-old boy is brought to play therapy by his parents due to a trauma he experienced at school. The mother reported that his teacher, who he was very close to, recently moved to another state. The school had not replaced the teacher yet and the class had several different substitutes. The mother stated he was sad when he had to go to school and he often stated he didn't like school anymore. The mother reported this was a significant change in his behavior since his teacher moved.

Excerpt from a Play Session

Reflection of Feeling

Child: (With a very sad voice.) I'm getting a new teacher because mine moved.

Therapist: You know you are getting a new teacher.

Commentary: This response is a reflection on content. Although the therapist's response is focused on the child, the therapist misses the opportunity to respond to emotion expressed by the child. If the therapist had responded to the feeling rather than the content, the session could move to a deeper level that helps the child learn to identify and verbally communicate her feelings.

Corrected Response

Child: (With a very sad voice.) I'm getting a new teacher because mine moved.

Therapist: You are sad your teacher moved and you miss her very much.

Commentary: This response validates the child's feelings and helps the child feel understood. This also helps build a trusting relationship between the child and the therapist. The therapist also communicates that the child's feelings are important.

CASE STUDY PRACTICE

Write a therapist response that is a reflection of feeling.

After you have written a response to each situation, turn to the next page and compare your responses with recommended play therapist responses. Resist the urge to look at the recommended responses before you write your own.

Child: (Picking up a toy from the shelf and turning toward the therapist.) I know what this is, I have one at home and they have one at school!

Therapist: _____

Child: I like to go to school because I get to play with my friend.

Therapist: _____

Child: (Goes to the chalkboard and begins to draw.) Yeah but sometimes we have to read.

Therapist: _____

Child: Uh huh. (Still drawing on the board.)

Therapist: _____

Child: I like to draw at school but I don't get to because the teacher said the board is just for her.

Therapist: _____

Child: We don't get to play what we want either. We have to do what the teacher says.

Therapist: _____

Child: (Begins to play in the sandbox.) I like this too.

Therapist: _____

Child: But when Mommy takes me to the park I can't play in the sand because I might get dirty.

Therapist: _____

Child: But sometimes I can play in the sand when Daddy takes me to the park.

Therapist: _____

Child: He doesn't get to go much because he has to work.

Therapist: _____

EXAMPLE: THERAPEUTIC RESPONSES THAT REFLECT FEELING

Child: (Picking up a toy from the shelf and turning toward the therapist.) I know what this is, I have one at home and they have one at school!

Therapist: You're excited to see some toys you use in other places.

Child: I like to go to school because I get to play with my friend.

Therapist: You like school and have fun with your friend.

Child: (Goes to the chalkboard and begins to draw.) Yeah but sometimes we have to read.

Therapist: Sounds like you don't like to have to read at school.

Child: Uh huh. (Still drawing on the board.)

Therapist: You are making something right on there . . . you are really concentrating on what you are drawing.

Child: Yeah . . . I like to draw at school but I don't get to because the teacher said the board is just for her.

Therapist: Sounds like you feel mad when you don't get to draw on the board at school.

Child: Yeah . . . we don't get to play what we want either. We have to do what the teacher says.

Therapist: You feel mad when you don't get to play at school.

Child: (Begins to play in the sandbox.) I like this too.

Therapist: You found something else you enjoy.

Child: Yeah . . . but when Mommy takes me to the park I can't play in the sand because I might get dirty.

Therapist: You feel disappointed when you can't play the way you want to at the park.

Child: But sometimes I can play in the sand when Daddy takes me to the park.

Therapist: You like going to the park with Daddy.

Child: He doesn't get to go much because he has to work.

Therapist: You feel sad when Daddy can't go to the park with you.

THERAPIST'S TONE OF VOICE AND EXPRESSION

Use your tone of voice to communicate meaning and feeling.

- Some people use a different tone of voice with young children. They may use a higher pitch voice or raise the pitch of their voice at the end of the sentence. This tone communicates an attitude that the child is not capable.

- A monotone voice communicates lack of interest in the child. The therapist who is being genuine allows his or her personality to shine. The therapist uses a conversational tone as is used with others in his or her daily interactions.

- When a child is not excited, and the therapist responds to the child in an overly excited voice, the child may think that something is wrong. The child also may distrust his or her own reaction since the child is not equally as excited.

  For example, a child is looking for the baby bottle and finds it. (The child does not appear excited.) The therapist responds "Wow! You found it!" This response communicates a sense of excitement that the child is not experiencing and therefore, may lead or structure the child's resulting behavior.

Personal Reflection: Reflect on your observations of adults talking with children. What are some of the effective and ineffective ways adults use to communicate with children.

_____

_____

_____

_____

Therapist's Tone of Voice and Expression Is Congruent with the Child's Affect

- During the play therapy session, children are developing a greater understanding of their feelings and themselves. When reflecting children's feelings or validating their experience, the therapist's tone of voice needs to mirror children's expressions and experiences.

The child is quiet and solemn while burying several people in the sand.

Inaccurate Reflection: In a happy or excited voice the therapist states: You know how to bury the people in the sand.

Accurate Reflection: In a solemn tone of voice the therapist states: You are burying them in the sand.

The child looks angry and is hitting and kicking the bop bag.

Inaccurate Reflection: In a quiet and sad voice the therapist states: Oh, no, you are really letting him have it. (Almost empathizing with Bobo's feelings.)

Accurate Reflection: In an angry voice the therapist states: You're really angry. You're letting him have it.

Personal Reflection: What emotions are most challenging for you to respond to in an empathic manner? How can you respond in an empathic manner and use a tone of voice congruent with the child's affect?

_____

_____

_____

_____

_____

Therapist's Tone of Voice and Expression Is Congruent with the Therapist's Responses

In a sad voice the child states that there has been an earthquake and all of the people have died.

Inaccurate Reflection:	In a light-hearted voice, the therapist states: You are sad that there has been an earthquake and all of the people have been killed.
Accurate Reflection:	In a sad tone of voice, the therapist states: You are sad that there has been an earthquake and all of the people have been killed.

- Although this may seem obvious, it is important to mirror the depth and intensity of the child's experience. Children use toys to express their feelings and thoughts. Their play is meaningful and is often representative of life experiences.

Personal Reflection: Describe a situation in which your tone of voice has not been congruent with the feelings you were acknowledging. How will you address this issue?

_____

_____

_____

_____

_____

_____

_____

_____

GUIDELINES FOR REFLECTING FEELINGS

1. Personalize the message by beginning the reflection with "you."

2. At the beginning of reflections, avoid repetitive use of phrases such as "sounds like."

3. Therapists need to be aware of feelings that they avoid or are uncomfortable dealing with in their personal lives. Sometimes these same feelings are difficult to acknowledge in the child.

Discussion Question: What do children learn when the play therapist reflects their feelings? How does the child then feel?

Discussion Question: What feelings do you avoid or what feelings are difficult for you to express?

Video Review and Reflection: Video a play therapy session you have with a child. Review the video and listen for responses that reflect feeling. Identify eight responses that do not contain adequate or accurate tone of voice. Explain how you think your tone of voice should be changed.

COMMENTS OR SUGGESTIONS THAT DIRECT CHILDREN

Instead of facilitating decision-making and responsibility, some therapists make comments or suggestions that direct children.

When a child takes charge in a situation and makes decisions about what he wants to do next, he learns to be more autonomous, independent, and may become more comfortable initiating his ideas.

Examples:

Child: The child enters the play room.

Therapist: Look at this dollhouse! You can create a story about the family.

Child: What should I paint?

Therapist: Paint a picture of your family.

These responses direct the child's behavior and eliminate an opportunity for the child to provide his own direction and/or make his own decisions.

Discussion Question: What does a child learn when the play therapist directs the child or makes suggestions?

Video Review and Reflection: Review a video of a play therapy session. Write down responses that lead or directed the child. Describe how these responses impacted the child.

CHAPTER 8

FACILITATING DECISION-MAKING AND RESPONSIBILITY

What is facilitating decision-making and responsibility?

- When children ask questions or seek assistance, the therapist will make a response that returns the responsibility to the child. These responses encourage children to make their own decisions and to take responsibility for a current concern.

Example:

Child: What should I play with first?

Therapist: In here, it's up to you to decide what you'd like to do.

Additional Examples of Responses that Facilitate Decision-Making

- That can be whatever you want it to be.

- You can paint that any color you want it to be.

- In here, you can spell that word any way you want.

Why facilitate decision-making and responsibility in a child?

- Children can learn how to make decisions and to take responsibility for themselves at a young age. These skills are developed throughout childhood and will prepare children to make decisions during the teen years and into adulthood.

- Children who are provided opportunities to learn decision-making and self-responsibility become self-directed, self-motivated, and feel a sense of control in their lives.

- Responsibility needs to be learned through experience. When adults make decisions for children that children are capable of making themselves, children are deprived of a learning opportunity. Instead of developing self-responsibility, children learn to become dependent upon the adult.

Why not automatically help a child when they ask for help?

- Children will learn that they are not capable, they may feel inadequate, and may become dependent upon an adult to accomplish a task that they could complete on their own. By readily completing tasks for children, the children are missing an opportunity to figure something out on their own. When children put effort into completing a task, they feel a sense of accomplishment and pride upon its completion.

Personal Reflection: Some beginning therapists feel a strong need to immediately assist a child who is struggling with a specific task. What beliefs might this therapist have about themselves as a helper and about children (or a person who is struggling)?

_____

_____

_____

_____

_____

_____

_____

_____

PRACTICE: FACILITATING DECISION-MAKING AND RESPONSIBILITY

1. The child holds up a toy and asks: "What is this used for?"

Response: _____.

2. The child enters the playroom for the first session, looks at the play therapist and asks: "What should I do?"

Response: _____.

3. The child picks up a dinosaur and asks: "What type of dinosaur is this?"

Response: _____.

4. The child is in the kitchen area cooking dinner and asks: "What should I make for dinner?"

Response: _____.

5. Without having made an effort to look, the child shows you a piece of crumbled paper and asks: "Where is the trash can?"

Response: _____.

6. A six-year-old child spills water on the floor and tells you: "Clean it up."

Response: _____.

Discussion Question: What do children learn when the play therapist responds in a way that facilitates decision-making? How does the child then feel?

Video Review and Reflection: Video a play therapy session you have with a child. Review the video and listen for responses that facilitate decision-making and responsibility. Identify eight opportunities you missed to facilitate decision-making. Use the following format to write responses you could have made.

Child: What the child said or did.

Therapist: Your response or note that no response was made.

Corrected Response: What you wish you had said.

Reason for Corrected Response: Explain why the corrected response is more effective and/or how it impacts the child.

EXAMPLE OF INEFFECTIVE AND EFFECTIVE RESPONSES THAT FACILITATE DECISION-MAKING

General Information

A six-year-old girl was brought to play therapy by her mother to help her transition into the school setting. The mother reported she was having difficulty at school with her teacher. The teacher reported to the mother that the girl had difficulty starting assignments during class and that she often asked for help even when she knew how to complete the work. The mother also stated that her daughter often looked for guidance and approval from her even on simple tasks at home.

Excerpt from a Play Session

Facilitation of Decision-Making:

Child:	(Picks up the toy medical kit.) What is this? How is it used?
Therapist:	That is a medical kit. You can pretend you are a doctor.
Child:	(Picks out the stethoscope.) What is this thing for? (Puts the stethoscope in her ears.)
Therapist:	You put it in your ears and listen to the heartbeat.
Commentary:	The therapist takes the lead in the session by answering the child's questions and goes into a teaching role rather than a therapeutic role. The therapist wants to facilitate the child's ability to make decisions and choices that are within the child's capabilities. In the playroom, the child is given the opportunity to explore the toys and use them in the ways that they want. This allows the child to develop their decision-making skills.

Corrected Response

Child: (Picks up the toy medical kit.) What is this? How is it used?

Therapist: You're trying to decide just how to use that.

Child: (Picks out the stethoscope.) What is this thing for? (Puts in her ears.)

Therapist: You are curious about it. Looks like you kncw how to use it.

Commentary: By allowing the child to explore the toys and decide how she wants to use them, the therapist encourages and facilitates the child's ability to make decisions.

CASE STUDY PRACTICE

Write a therapist response to facilitate decision-making.

After you have written a response to each situation, turn to the next page and compare your responses with recommended play therapist responses. Resist the urge to look at the recommended responses before you write your own.

Child: (Enters the playroom and looks around the room.) What should I do?

Therapist: _____

Child: (Walks toward the arts and crafts table and pulls out a piece of paper.) I know what I can do.

Therapist: _____

Child: I am gonna make a picture for my mommy.

Therapist: _____

Child: (Begins to pick out colors from the markers/crayons and starts drawing.)

Therapist: _____

Child: I'm gonna make a rainbow.

Therapist: _____

Child: Yeah . . . what colors should I put in my rainbow?

Therapist: _____

Child: I think I'll use blue and red because they are my favorite colors.

Therapist: _____

Child: Now I'm gonna make some flowers.

Therapist: _____

Child: (Begins to draw the flowers.)

Therapist: _____

Child: (Brings the picture to therapist.) All done. I am gonna give this to Mommy.

Therapist: _____

EXAMPLE: THERAPIST RESPONSES FOR FACILITATING DECISION-MAKING

Child: (Enters the playroom and looks around the room.) What should I do?

Therapist: **In here you can decide what you want to play.**

Child: (Walks toward the arts and crafts table and pulls out a piece of paper.) I know what I can do.

Therapist: **You figured out what you want to do.**

Child: I am gonna make a picture for my mommy.

Therapist: **You've got a plan and know just what you want to do.**

Child: (Begins to pick out colors from the markers/crayons and starts drawing.) I'm gonna make a rainbow.

Therapist: **You know just what you want to do and how to make it.**

Child: Yeah . . . what colors should I put in my rainbow?

Therapist: **You can decide what colors to use.**

Child: I think I'll use blue and red because they are my favorite colors.

Therapist: **You figured out a way to decide what colors to use.**

Child: Now I'm gonna make some flowers.

Therapist: **Decided what you wanted to draw next.**

Child: (Begins to draw the flowers.)

Therapist: **You are working hard on your picture.**

Child: (Brings the picture to the therapist.) All done. I am gonna give this to Mommy.

Therapist: **You got it just the way you want it and are excited to give it to your mommy.**

GUIDELINES FOR HELPING A CHILD

1. When you see a child struggling to complete a task, don't jump in to help. Wait until the child asks for help.

   Encourage the child while he or she is working on the task:

   - You are really working hard to get that done.

   - You are figuring out a way to get that open.

2. Especially encourage the child to complete age-appropriate tasks on his own.

   For example, a three-year-old child may have difficulty taking off a lid that has been tightly put on a plastic jar. It is appropriate to work together as a team to open the jar lid.

3. Don't help a child who has not made an attempt at the task and asks for help.

4. If a child:

   a. Tried to accomplish the task

   b. Asked you for help

   c. And the task seems challenging for someone his or her age

   Then, respond: "Show me what you want done."

- This response encourages the child to make decisions about how the child would like you to help. This approach also helps the child focus on what specifically needs to be done to accomplish the task.

While working on the task together:

- Encourage the child — "You are working hard . . . "

Upon completion of the task:

- You did it. You got that off. (Instead of: We did it. We got that off.)

- Place the focus on the child and the child's accomplishment.

Write a response for each child who is seeking help.

1. The child is struggling to get a knot untied from the piece of rope. The child asks you to help.

Response: _____

2. You and the child successfully complete a task that you were working on together.

Response: _____

3. The four-year-old child grabs the handcuffs, brings them to you, and asks "will you open these?"

Response: _____

4. The child is struggling to get the doll's jacket zipped.

Response: _____

Discussion Question: What does the child learn when the play therapist encourages the child to accomplish a task on her own? How does the child then feel?

Video Review and Reflection: Video a play therapy session you have with a child. Review the video and identify times that you helped the child. Did you encourage the child to attempt the task on his or her own? Identify times when you helped the child and wish you responded differently. Use the following format to write responses you could have made.

Child: What the child said or did.

Therapist: Your response or note that no response was made.

Corrected Response: What you wish you had said.

Reason for Corrected Response: Explain why the corrected response is more effective and/or how it impacts the child.

PRAISE OR JUDGMENT STATEMENTS

Examples of Praise and Judgment Statements

Great job!	What a beautiful picture.
You're such a good boy.	That looks awesome.
You're good at that.	What a fantastic tower.

- Some people feel that praise is a positive way to reinforce children's abilities and behavior. However, children may become dependent on receiving praise in order to feel good and may constantly seek approval and strive to please others.

- Children who are encouraged to value the effort and work they put toward an accomplishment develop an internal source of evaluation. Instead of looking for the approval of others, they are able to applaud their own effort and accomplishments.

- The adult providing praise or judgment is in a position of power and evaluation. This adult has the power to provide or deny praise and make positive or negative judgments. This encourages the development of an external locus of control. The child learns to allow others' ideas and beliefs to direct his or her life.

- Praise structures or reinforces a child to produce or do more of the same.

- A child who receives encouragement is more likely to develop an internal locus of control and to become self-directed and self-responsible.

CHAPTER 9

FACILITATING ESTEEM-BUILDING AND ENCOURAGEMENT

The following section discusses the difference between praise and encouragement and describes how to make encouraging statements that facilitate esteem-building.

Rationale for Making Encouraging Statements Instead of Statements of Praise:

> Children will learn to become self-motivated and will not look for others' praise and comments to determine self-worth.

The Difference between Praise and Encouragement

PRAISE

Praise judges a child's abilities and self-worth. It tells the child what *you* think about his or her abilities. It teaches the child to value the "self" based upon other's positive and negative comments.

STATEMENT OF PRAISE

Therapist's Response: That's a beautiful picture!

Avoid this type of response. If a child can make a beautiful picture, they can also make a picture that displeases the therapist. Praise reinforces the child's need for a positive external locus of evaluation.

ENCOURAGEMENT

An encouraging response acknowledges the child's effort. It helps a child develop internal motivation and to value him or herself.

STATEMENT OF ENCOURAGEMENT

Therapist's Response: You worked hard on that picture.

Rationale for Using Encouraging Responses:

This type of response helps a child learn to give credit to him or herself and to appreciate his or her own abilities. This child will learn to be proud of self and will not formulate ideas about self-concept solely based upon other's evaluation.

EXAMPLES

- The child cooks dinner and hands you a plate with a pretend chicken leg on it. The child then asks, how do you like it?

Praise Response: This dinner is delicious!

- This response evaluates and judges the cook's performance. This encourages the child to be motivated by your comments and praise.

Encouraging Response: You worked hard making this dinner just for me.
(Show admiration in tone of voice.)

- This response focuses on the child's work and effort. It encourages the child to develop internal motivation. The child will become self-motivated instead of relying on praise from others.

ENCOURAGING COMMENTS

You know how to:

count, feed the baby, build the blocks, write your name, etc.

The statement "you know how to" reflects ability instead of making a judgment as to the child's ability (i.e., you're good at counting).

OTHER ENCOURAGING COMMENTS

You are making it just the way you want.

You did it.

You got it.

You are trying hard.

You worked hard.

You really like your (picture).

You know just how you want it to go.

You are proud of (your tower).

Sounds like you know a lot about (dinsosaurs).

Personal Reflection: Describe praise and the effects of praise on children. Describe encouragement and the effects of encouragement on children.

_____

_____

_____

_____

_____

_____

_____

_____

PRACTICE IDENTIFYING STATEMENTS OF PRAISE AND ENCOURAGEMENT

Identify whether the following statements are statements of praise or encouragement.

1. You did such a great job making that tower.

   Praise   Encouragement

2. You worked really hard to make that tower.

   Praise   Encouragement

3. You like the way your picture came out. You spent a lot of time on it and used so many different colors.

   Praise   Encouragement

4. You're being such a good boy.

   Praise   Encouragement

5. You put a lot of effort into getting that off. You're proud that you did it without any help.

   Praise   Encouragement

6. That is such a beautiful picture.

   Praise   Encouragement

7. I'm proud of you.

   Praise   Encouragement

PRACTICE FACILITATING ESTEEM-BUILDING AND ENCOURAGEMENT

The child paints a picture, looks at you, and asks if you like it.

Response: _____

The child spent a long time setting up the toy soldiers.

Response: _____

The child has been figuring out how to open the handcuffs. After several minutes the child opens the handcuffs.

Response: _____

The child has put a lot of time and energy into setting up the dollhouse. When the child finishes setting up, your child says, "There."

Response: _____

Discussion Question: What does a child learn from esteem-building and encouraging comments? How does the child then feel?

Video Review and Reflection: Video a play therapy session you have with a child. Review the video and listen for responses that encourage and facilitate esteem-building. Identify eight times when you missed an opportunity to facilitate esteem-building. Use the following format to record responses.

Child: What the child said or did.

Therapist: Your response or note that no response was made.

Corrected Response: What you wish you had said.

Reason for Corrected Response: Explain why the corrected response is more effective and/or how it impacts the child.

What are your strengths in utilizing this skill? What would you like to improve upon or change? What questions do you have about using this skill?

EXAMPLES OF INEFFECTIVE AND EFFECTIVE RESPONSES THAT ENCOURAGE AND FACILITATE ESTEEM-BUILDING

Praise and Evaluation versus Encouragement and Esteem-Building

One goal of therapy is for the child to build esteem by internalizing her own positive statements about herself. Praise is being defined as nondescriptive evaluative statements containing words such as wonderful, good, great, beautiful. These words evaluate the child or the child's product (a painting, block tower). The evaluator holds the power and the child learns to need additional praise in order to feel good about herself. This type of praise does not make a positive long-term impact on the child because it lacks description. If the child relies on external praise and evaluations, her peers, family members, and other adults' comments define what she thinks and how she feels about herself.

On the other hand, comments that acknowledge time, effort, and hard work describe the process of creating a picture or block tower. This type of message can be internalized. "I worked hard to make this tower." Thus, the therapist's recognition of efforts and hard work can be integrated into the child's self-concept and beliefs about herself. The child learns to acknowledge her own personal qualities, commitment, and effort.

General Information

Jared's father, Marc, brought eight-year-old Jared into play therapy because he was having difficulty making friends at home and at school. Jared complained that all the neighborhood children were making fun of him and that his teacher and the kids at school did not like him.

Excerpt from the Fourth Play Therapy Session with Tyler

During the first three play therapy sessions, the therapist noticed that Jared looked for verbal acceptance and reassurance frequently throughout the session. Although the therapist understood the philosophical difference between esteem-building and evaluation and praise, she began to praise and evaluate Jared in order to help him develop a stronger self-concept.

Excerpt #1

Child: "Look at this picture I made! Do you like it?"

Therapist: "Your picture is awesome."

Corrected Response

Child: "Look at this picture I made! Do you like it?"

Therapist: "You worked very hard on your picture. You sound excited about the way it turned out."

Child: "But do you like it?"

Therapist: "It's important for you to know what I think. What is really important is what you think. Jared, you're proud of the picture you made. You put a lot of effort into making it."

Commentary

Jared is looking to the therapist for approval and positive evaluation. By providing general positive evaluation, the child is receiving a message that the therapist thinks his picture is "awesome." Although this evaluation was positive, Jared may worry that future evaluations may be negative. If all the therapist's evaluations are positive, Jared may doubt the authenticity of his relationship with the therapist. By avoiding evaluation, the therapist creates an environment of acceptance that is not based on Jared's performance.

Instead of evaluating the outcome, the therapist is teaching the child to acknowledge the time and effort put into creating the picture. If Jared believes that he put a lot of time and effort into creating his picture, he will be able to internalize this message and applaud himself for his efforts. However, it is not possible for Jared to internalize an external message that a picture is beautiful. Instead, he hears the message that my therapist thinks my picture is beautiful. Thus, it remains important for Jared to gain others, praise and approval in order to feel good about himself.

Excerpt # 2

Child:
Jared described each dinosaur. He told the therapist "I know what each dinosaur is called and can tell you if it is a carnivore or not."

Therapist:
"You are very smart."

Commentary:
The therapist's response communicates that the therapist thinks Jared is intelligent. This response does not give Jared an opportunity to internalize the message that he is smart. It is an external evaluation. If Jared believes the therapist's words then he is learning that the therapist thinks he is smart. There is no opportunity for Jared to evaluate himself as smart.

Corrected Response

Child:
Jared described each dinosaur. He told the therapist "I know what each dinosaur is called and can tell you if it is a carnivore or not."

Therapist:
"You know a lot about dinosaurs. You know their names and whether or not they are meat eaters."

Commentary:
Instead of making a general evaluation of the child, the therapist acknowledges the child's knowledge and abilities. Since the therapist's response specifically describes the child's abilities, the child is able to internalize this type of message. Jared can say to himself "I do know a lot about dinosaurs." By internalizing this message, Jared validates his own knowledge about dinosaurs.

CASE STUDY PRACTICE

Write therapist responses using esteem-building and encouraging responses.

After you have written a response to each situation, turn to the next page and compare your responses with recommended play therapist responses. Resist the urge to look at the recommended responses before you write your own.

Child: (Child builds a very tall tower out of blocks.) Look at this. Isn't it awesome?

Therapist: _____

Child: Yeah. But what do you think of the tower?

Therapist: _____

Child: I am proud of my tower. (Walks over to the chalkboard and begins to write multiplication problems on the board.) I know how to do multiplication.

Therapist: _____

Child: Child multiplies the numbers 20 times 20. (Writes the answer 400 under the problem.) Look at this! (Pride in voice.)

Therapist: _____

Child: (Writes another multiplication problem and the answer.) I had to do so many worksheets for homework before I could do this.

Therapist: _____

Child: Yes. It seemed like I spent hours learning it. At times it seemed so difficult, I just wanted to give up and go outside and play.

Therapist: _____

Child: My dad says to never give up and I agree.

Therapist: _____

Child: (Walks over to the easel and starts to paint.) I'm not very good at painting pictures.

Therapist: _____

Child: I really want to be a better painter.

Therapist: _____

Child: (Paints a picture of a house and looks at the therapist.) Well, what do you think of that?

Therapist: _____

EXAMPLE: THERAPEUTIC RESPONSES FOR FACILITATING ENCOURAGEMENT AND ESTEEM-BUILDING

Child: (Child builds a very tall tower out of blocks.) Look at this. Isn't it awesome?

Therapist: You really like the way it turned out.

Child: Yeah. But what do you think of the tower?

Therapist: You put a lot of time into making it and you look proud of your work.

Child: I am proud of my tower. (Walks over to the chalkboard and begins to write multiplication problems on the board.) I know how to do multiplication.

Therapist: You know how to multiply numbers.

Child: Child multiplies the numbers 20 times 20. (Writes the answer 400 under the problem.) Look at this! (Pride in voice.)

Therapist: You're excited and proud of your ability to do multiplication.

Child: (Writes another multiplication problem and the answer.) I had to do so many worksheets for homework before I could do this.

Therapist: You put a lot of work and effort into learning how to do multiplication.

Child: Yes. It seemed like I spent hours learning it. At times it seemed so difficult, I just wanted to give up and go outside and play.

Therapist: Even though it was very difficult, you kept trying and trying and you didn't give up.

Child: My dad says to never give up and I agree.

Therapist: You believe that if you try hard enough you can accomplish lots of different things.

Child: (Walks over to the easel and starts to paint.) I'm not very good at painting pictures.

Therapist: You're not sure about painting but you're still going to paint.

Child: I really want to be a better painter.

Therapist: Painting is one of those things you'd like to improve.

Child: (Paints a picture of a house and looks at the therapist.) Well, what do you think of that?

Therapist: You used lots of different colors. You made windows, curtains, and a window in your door and a doorknob. You also made trees and flowers outside your house.

SETTING LIMITS

Limits are set to:

- Protect the child
- Protect the therapist
- Protect the toys and the room
- Anchor the session to reality
- Structure the session
- Limit socially unacceptable behavior
- Help child learn self-control

Why set limits?

- Limit-setting ensures a safe and secure environment for children.
- Limit-setting teaches self-control and self-responsibility.

When to set limits

- Children are not permitted to hurt themselves or the therapist.
- Limits are used to protect the playroom and the toys.

How to set limits

- Set limits in a consistent manner. Consistent limits create the structure for a consistent environment.
- Use a calm, patient, and firm voice.
- Limits set quickly communicate anxiety and lack of trust toward the child.

Discussion: Discuss the different messages that are implied in the following limit-setting statements?

UNDERSTANDING MESSAGES SENT WHEN SETTING LIMITS

Briefly describe the underlying message that is being sent to the child in each situation.

- It's probably not a good idea to paint the wall.

Message: _____

- We can't paint the walls in here.

Message: _____

- You shouldn't paint the wall.

Message: _____

- I can't let you paint the wall.

Message: _____

- The rule is you can't paint the wall.

Message: _____

- The wall is not for painting on.

Message: _____

THREE STEPS TO LIMIT-SETTING (ACT)
Landreth, 2002

A   Acknowledge the Feeling

- Using the child's name will help the play therapist get the child's attention.

- By acknowledging the child's feeling, the play therapist is communicating understanding and acceptance of the child's feeling.

- Communicating understanding of the feeling frequently defuses the intensity of the feeling.

- All feelings, desires, and wishes are accepted but not all behaviors.

C   Communicate the Limit

- Be specific, clear, and exact about the limit.

- Debates and long explanations are avoided.

- Unclear limits make it difficult for the child to act responsibly.

The wall is not for painting versus You can't put a lot of paint on that wall.

T   Target an Alternative

- Provide an alternative to the child so that the child can express the original action.

- The wall is not for coloring on; the paper is for coloring on. (Therapist points toward paper).

- The child is confronted with a choice. (Choosing the original action or the targeted alternative.) The child is provided with an opportunity to exercise self-control.

EXAMPLE

The child is painting a picture and begins painting the chair.

A I know you'd like to paint that.

C The chair is not for painting.

T You can paint on the paper (points toward the paper).

PRACTICE SETTING LIMITS

---

1. The child begins to color on the dollhouse.

A I know you really want to _____

C But the dollhouse _____

T The paper is _____

2. The child aims a loaded dart gun at you.

A _____

C _____

T _____

3. The child begins to throw a plastic ball as hard as possible at the light fixture.

A _____

C _____

T _____

4. After fifteen minutes in the playroom, the child announces that she wants to leave and go outside to see her mother.

A _____

C _____

T _____

5. The child wants to play doctor and asks you to be the patient. The child asks you to unbutton your shirt so that she/he can listen to your heart.

A _____

C _____

T _____

6. The child went to the bathroom prior to beginning the play session. During the session, the child asks to leave the room to go to the water fountain. Ten minutes later, the child asks to get another drink.

(Limit — one trip to get a drink or go to the bathroom per session.)

A _____

C _____

T _____

7. Describe a situation in which you would need to set a limit during the play session.

Situation: _____

_____

A _____

C _____

T _____

Discussion Question: What does a child learn when the play therapist sets limits? How does the child then feel?

Video Review and Reflection: Review a video of a play therapy session. Listen and observe limit-setting. Was the ACT model used? If one part of the three-step model was left out, how did this impact the child's response?

Video Review and Reflection: Video a play therapy session you have with a child. Review the video and listen for limit-setting responses. Identify missed opportunities to set limits using the ACT model. Use the following format to record responses.

Child: What the child said or did.

Therapist: Your response or note that no response was made.

Corrected Response: What you wish you had said.

Reason for Corrected Response: Explain why the corrected response is more effective and/or how it impacts the child.

What are your strengths in utilizing this skill? What would you like to improve upon or change? What questions do you have about using this skill?

EXAMPLES OF INEFFECTIVE AND EFFECTIVE
LIMIT-SETTING USING THE ACT MODEL

General Information

Jenna's mother, Sue, brought five-year-old Jenna to play therapy. Sue reported that she had "difficulty getting Jenna to listen." Sue explained that Jenna had frequent "tantrums" in which she screamed and cried for long periods of time, threw toys around the room, and tried to slap her.

Excerpt from the Second Play Therapy Session with Jenna

Child: "I don't like these dinosaurs." (Tone of voice sounded angry.) Jenna picked up the dinosaur and threw it across the room. Then, she grabbed the plastic bat and began to hit the dinosaur. After hitting the dinosaur approximately ten times, Jenna picked up the dinosaur and threw it at the glass window.

Therapist: "Jenna, I can't let you throw the dinosaur at the window. It is expensive and may break."

Commentary: The therapist stated that she can't let Jenna throw the dinosaur at the window. This statement communicates that the therapist is responsible for enforcing what Jenna can and cannot do. Instead, the therapist wants Jenna to become responsible for her c. . actions.

The therapist also failed to acknowledge Jenna's feelings of anger. The validation of Jenna's feelings helps Jenna feel understood and helps build a trusting relationship between Jenna and the therapist. The therapist also wants to communicate that Jenna's feelings are important. By verbally acknowledging Jenna's feelings of anger, the therapist helps increase Jenna's personal awareness of her feelings and helps her learn to identify and verbally communicate her feelings to others.

The therapist did not target an alternative means for Jenna to express her anger. By communicating another way to express her anger, the therapist provides a means for Jenna to get her needs met while maintaining an environment of safety in the playroom.

Additional Information

During the parent consultation with Sue, Jenna's mother, Sue stated that Jenna frequently does not listen and that she becomes exhausted by the numerous requests. Sue explained that she often tries to ignore Jenna's behavior. For example, Sue stated that even though Jenna is not allowed to have cookies before dinner, she will repeatedly ask for a cookie. Sue initially tells her "no" and then begins ignoring her requests. After Jenna repeats the request several times, Sue reports "giving in and giving Jenna a cookie." Jenna has learned that if she makes the request repeatedly, she will get a cookie.

The therapist understands that Jenna may challenge limits and experience difficulty responding to limits in the playroom. The therapist's goal is to provide a safe environment by protecting Jenna, the therapist, the playroom, and playroom materials. The therapist also wants to acknowledge Jenna's feelings and provide an alternative way to express herself. The therapist wants to help Jenna learn self-control without Jenna feeling personally rejected.

Corrected Response

Child: "I don't like these dinosaurs." (Tone of voice sounded angry.) Jenna picked up the dinosaur and threw it across the room. She grabbed the plastic bat and began to hit the dinosaur. Jenna picked up the dinosaur and threw it at the glass window.

Therapist: Therapist uses the ACT model to set a limit as soon as Jenna begins throwing the dinosaur across the room. "Jenna, you sound very angry at the dinosaurs. The toys are not for throwing. You can make a dinosaur out of Play-Doh and smash it with your hands."

In this example, the therapist used the ACT model to acknowledge Jenna's feelings, communicate the limit, and target an alternative.

Acknowledge Feelings   "You sound very angry at the dinosaurs."

Communicate the Limit   "The toys are not for throwing."

Target an Alternative   "You can make a dinosaur out of Play-Doh and smash it with your hands."

Commentary: First, the therapist immediately acknowledged Jenna's feelings of anger. This helps Jenna become aware of and learn to verbalize her feelings of anger. By clearly communicating the limit "toys are not for throwing," the therapist helps Jenna learn the playroom guidelines and provides her an opportunity to accept responsibility for her behavior. Lastly, the therapist provides an alternative means for Jenna to express her anger in a way that is not harmful to herself, others, the playroom or the materials.

CASE STUDY PRACTICE

Write the therapist's responses for setting limits.

After you have written a response to each situation, turn to the next page and compare your responses with recommended play therapist responses. Resist the urge to look at the recommended responses before you write your own.

Child: (The child appears excited. She walks over to the easel, puts yellow paint on a brush, and begins to paint the floor tile.)

Therapist: _____

Child: (Kailey stands up, looks at the therapist and puts the paintbrush in the red paint. She bends down and begins painting the floor tile.)

Therapist: _____

Child: (Kailey's facial expression appears angry. She throws the paintbrush at the easel and walks over to the sandbox.)

Therapist: _____

Child: I am angry. I don't like you. I want to leave and see my mommy right now.

Therapist: _____

Child: You're not my mom. You can't tell me what to do. (Walks over to the easel, grabs the container of red paint, and begins pouring it into the sandbox.)

Therapist: _____

Child: (Kailey scoops up the red sand and puts it into the bucket. She dumps a little more red paint into the bucket and mixes it.) I'd like to throw this right on top of your head. You have too many rules in here.

Therapist: _____

Child: Really . . . All right! Now, this is fun. (Finishes emptying the bucket and walks over to the sink. Looks at the therapist and smiles.) I'm going to wash my hands. (Kailey puts on the water, laughs, and begins splashing water onto the floor and the walls near the sink.)

Therapist: _____

Child: You are no fun. Can't I do anything in here? (Walks over to the shelf, picks up the plastic dart gun, loads it, and aims it at the therapist.) Just be quiet!

Therapist: _____

Child: (Continues to point the loaded gun at the therapist and shoots.) No one tells me what to do. Not even my mother.

Therapist: _____

Child: I don't like following rules. (Kailey loads the plastic dart gun again and shoots at the therapist.)

Therapist: _____

EXAMPLE: THERAPEUTIC RESPONSES FOR LIMIT SETTING

Child: (The child appears excited. She walks over to the easel, puts yellow paint on a brush, and begins to paint the floor tile.)

Therapist: Kailey, you seem excited to paint the floor but the floor is not for painting. The paper is for painting on.

Child: (Kailey stands up, looks at the therapist, and puts the paintbrush in the red paint. She bends down and begins painting the floor tile.)

Therapist: Kailey, I know that you really want to paint the floor, but the floor is not for painting. The paper on the easel is for painting.

Child: (Kailey's facial expression appears angry. She throws the paintbrush at the easel and walks over to the sandbox.)

Therapist: You're angry that I said the floor is not for painting.

Child: I am angry. I don't like you. I want to leave and see my mommy right now.

Therapist: You're so angry that you wish you could leave this very minute. But our time is not up for today. We have forty more minutes in the playroom and then you can go see your mommy.

Child: You're not my mom. You can't tell me what to do. Walks over to the easel, grabs the container of red paint, and begins pouring it into the sandbox.

Therapist: You're really angry. The paint is not for pouring into the sandbox. Paint and sand can be put into the sand bucket and mixed together.

Child: (Kailey scoops up the red sand and puts it into the bucket. She dumps a little more red paint into the bucket and mixes it.) I'd like to throw this right on top of your head. You have too many rules in here.

Therapist: You're angry with me. You don't like the rules in here, but I'm not for pouring sand on. You can pour that red sand into the trash can and pretend you're pouring it on my head.

Child:	Really . . . All right! Now, this is fun. (Finishes emptying the bucket and walks over to the sink. Looks at the therapist and smiles.) I'm going to wash my hands. (Kailey puts on the water, laughs, and begins splashing water onto the floor and the walls near the sink.)
Therapist:	**Kailey, you like splashing the water all over, but the water is for keeping in the sink. You can pretend you're splashing water all over the room.**
Child:	You are no fun. Can't I do anything in here? (Walks over to the shelf, picks up the plastic dart gun, loads it, and aims it at the therapist.) Just be quiet!
Therapist:	**I'm not for shooting. You can shoot at the bop bag and pretend it's me. You're tired of hearing about the things you can't do.**
Child:	(Continues to point the loaded gun at the therapist and shoots.) No one tells me what to do. Not even my mother.
Therapist:	**(Therapist holds out her hand to block the plastic dart.) You don't like anyone telling you what to do but I'm not for shooting. You can shoot at the bop bag and pretend it's me.**
Child:	I don't like following rules. (Kailey loads the plastic dart gun again and shoots at the therapist.)
Therapist:	**Kailey, if you choose to shoot at the bop bag or the walls, you choose to continue playing with the dart gun. If you choose to shoot the dart gun at me, you choose not to play with the dart gun for the rest of our time today.**

CHAPTER 11

UNDERSTANDING THERAPEUTIC RESPONSES, PLAY BEHAVIORS, FACILITATING HEALING, AND TERMINATION

ENHANCING THERAPEUTIC RESPONSES

1. Make responses short.

- Short responses are easier to follow than lengthy responses.

2. Make responses interactive.

- Responses that are interactive and flow like a conversation sound more natural and genuine.

3. Use an appropriate rate of responses.

- The child may feel overwhelmed when responses are too frequent.
- The child may feel watched if there is a lack of responses.
- An appropriate rate of responses will sound natural and conversational.

4. Make immediate and spontaneous responses.

- Immediate responses increase the child's awareness of his or her current feelings, behavior, or experience.
- Responses that are delayed may encourage the child to continue a behavior that the child was ready to discontinue.

Additional Guidelines

1. **When responding to a child, begin with the word "you" instead of using the child's name.**

a. Using the word "you" personalizes the message.

   Response: You like drawing that picture.

b. Using the child's name makes the child a non-person.

   Response: Robert likes drawing that picture.

2. **During the play therapy session the child is in the lead. Refrain from asking questions, answering questions, or teaching.**

a. Adults are usually in the position of being "the expert." Children look to adults for direction, permission, and answers. During the play session, the adult is not in the role of the teacher or a person who corrects children's responses. During play therapy, children are able to call a "giraffe" a "horse" without being corrected.

b. The child can add 5 plus 1 and get an answer of 7. In addition, the child can choose to spell any way the child decides. This is an accepting and permissive environment. The child can learn spelling and addition outside the play therapy session.

3. **When responding to the child use the word "you" instead of "we."**

"Sometimes we get upset when we paint something and it doesn't come out the way we want it to."

This takes the focus off of the child.

Instead: "You are upset that your painting didn't come out the way you wanted it to."

4. **Recognize the child's feelings.**

Absence of recognition of a child's feelings may be interpreted that such feelings are not acceptable. Validating the child's feelings helps the child identify and communicate feelings.

UNDERSTANDING CHILDREN'S PLAY BEHAVIORS

THEMES

What is a theme?

A theme is an inner emotional dynamic that the child expresses through her play. She may work through an emotional experience by repeating a specific play behavior, or play may be different but have similar meaning, or the child may repeatedly verbalize a story or event. The following is a list of common themes in children's play. However, many other themes emerge during a child's work besides the common themes listed below.

1. Exploratory

When a child first enters a new environment, she will spend time becoming familiar with her surroundings. She may work briefly with a toy before moving on to another toy or object in the playroom.

2. Relationship-Building

The way the child builds his relationship with the play therapist may be indicative of how he relates to other adults. He may build his relationship with the play therapist through seeking approval, or being manipulative, collaborative, or competitive. He also may test limits to learn the guidelines for being in this particular environment and with the therapist.

3. Mastery/Competence

A child strives to develop new competencies daily. In the play therapy room, she will use toys such as building blocks, artwork, ring toss, bowling, and sports equipment to improve skills and develop a sense of mastery. A child who is experiencing difficulty with schoolwork may use the chalkboard to write spelling words and/or mathematical equations to express her struggle and/or frustration in her learning environment. She may show competency through displaying words she knows how to spell and equations for which she knows the answers.

4. Power/Control

A child may be in an environment or situation in which he feels powerless. In the playroom, the child may execute power through locking up the "bad guy" and taking him to jail. A child may play the role of a teacher, principal, or parent who is reprimanding a child for misbehaving. The child may use words and phrases that have been directed toward him from adults in whose presence he has felt powerless.

5. Safety and Security

A child may desire a feeling of safety and security from adults and situations in his environment. For example, a child who has repeatedly watched the news broadcast of the aftermath of a tornado may act out preparing for the tornado and getting to a safe place. Another child may manipulate adults to get what he wants. As a result, he feels powerful over adults in his life and unsafe. He may present opportunities for the play therapist to set limits and to create the safe and secure environment he needs outside the playroom.

6. Nurturance

A child may act out the need for nurturance through preparing a meal in the kitchen, cuddling and caring for a baby doll, or by using the medical kit to care for someone who is sick or has been hurt.

7. Aggression/Revenge

A child may express aggression toward a stuffed animal, a bop bag, or toward the therapist. Some beginning play therapists find the intensity of aggression in young children startling. It is important to acknowledge the child's feelings and to only set limits when her behavior is hurtful to herself, the therapist, toys, or room.

8. Death/Loss/Grief

A child may experience loss and grief from moving to another home or school, through a divorce or a separation from family members, and through the death of a family member, friend, or pet. Some of the ways a child may express loss and grief include artwork, through burying dolls/objects in the sandbox, and through doll play.

9. Sexualized

A child who has been sexually abused and/or been exposed to pornographic medium may show excessive interest in sexual issues and/or victimization through artwork, discussion, and doll play.

THERAPEUTIC CHANGE AND HEALING

Through providing the core conditions and using the therapeutic responses in this manual, the child is empowered in the following ways:

1. The play therapist provides a caring, empathic, and safe environment. The child experiences acceptance, positive regard, and respect. The play therapist communicates "I am here. I hear you. I understand. I care. I believe in you."

• Some play therapists underestimate the power of the therapeutic relationship.

• How frequently are children in the presence of an adult who listens completely, shows a constant interest in the child's world, is understanding, does not judge or direct the child or help with tasks that the child is capable of accomplishing?

2. The therapeutic response of "Facilitating Decision-Making and Self-Responsibility" helps the child learn to take initiative, to make decisions, and problem-solve without immediately looking for assistance. Through having an adult communicate trust in the child's ability to make decisions, the child learns to trust himself and to take responsibility for his behavior.

3. "Esteem-Building" responses encourage a child to identify her strengths and internalize the message "I am capable" into her self-concept. By internalizing this message, she learns to value herself and to identify specific strengths and abilities. Also, she develops an internal source of evaluation and is less likely to engage in behaviors for the purpose of receiving praise and approval from others. Instead, she looks to herself for approval and feels proud and accepting of who she is.

4. A therapeutic response that reflects and acknowledges a child's feelings communicates acceptance of the child and his feelings. A child who is taught certain feelings are inappropriate may lose access to these emotions. He may shut down emotionally and/or think that emotional expression of a particular feeling makes him weak or unacceptable. Through reflecting feelings, the play therapist helps the child become aware of his feelings and to identify and express his feelings. In this process, the child learns to express feelings in ways that are not harmful to himself or others.

5. The ACT Model of setting limits helps a child internalize her own behavioral guidelines. Instead of being told exactly what to do, she is provided information and options and an opportunity to make a choice. For example, she is given information (the walls aren't for writing on) and is provided an alternative way to meet her needs (the paper is for writing on).

   This model eliminates possible power struggles between adults and children. Adults who believe that a child should always listen to them and follow their directives frequently feel frustrated by a child that perceives the adult statement as a challenge.

   Statements such as: "Don't write on those walls" creates a desire in some children to find out what will happen once they write on the walls. A child who is disciplined in this manner learns that she only has to behave when someone is present to reinforce the rules.

   The ACT model and the choice-giving model encourages the child to make choices and to develop an ability to set limits for herself. In addition, other adults in her life may be permissive and provide very few guidelines. Limits help her feel she is in a safe, consistent, and secure environment.

TERMINATION

Assessing Progress in the Child's Healing

- Growth and change may be a slow process

- Observe change in the child's playroom behavior

- Observe the first time a change has occurred

    For example: Patti painted pictures of a tornado for five sessions. During the sixth session and for the first time, instead of painting a tornado, she painted her and her friends running on the playground.

When is the child ready to end play therapy sessions?

Observe self-initiated changes in the child's behavior to help assess whether or not a child may be ready to terminate the therapeutic relationship.

Self-Initiated Changes that May Indicate Readiness to Terminate the Therapeutic Relationship (Landreth, 2002)

1. The child is less dependent and is able to focus on self.

2. The child expresses needs openly and is less confused.

3. The child accepts responsibility for own feelings and actions.

4. The child limits own behavior appropriately.

5. The child is more inner directed and initiates activities with assurance.

6. The child is flexible and tolerant of happenings.

7. The child is cooperative but not conforming.

8. The child has moved from negative-sad affect to happy-pleased affect.

9. The child is able to play out story sequences; play has direction.

10. The child is more accepting of self.

Ending the Therapeutic Relationship

- The child needs approximately 2 to 3 sessions in the playroom to explore feelings and concerns about ending therapy and the therapeutic relationship.

- The child should be included in the decision regarding when to end therapy.

- Once the decision has been made to end therapy, the therapist will remind the child at the end of each session:

Josh, we have two more times together in the playroom.

Josh, we have one more time together in the playroom.

Josh, this is our last time together (for now) in the playroom.

CHAPTER 12

TEACHING PARENTS HOW TO HELP THEIR CHILDREN DEVELOP SELF-CONTROL AND SELF-DISCIPLINE

The play therapist will be consulting with the parent(s) on a regular basis while the child is attending play therapy sessions. Many parents request information to help their children develop self-control and self-discipline. The following information can be used to help parents learn new skills for working with their children.

GIVING A CHOICE BETWEEN TWO ALTERNATIVES

Rationale for Giving Choices

Providing children with choices that are age appropriate gives children an opportunity to make decisions and take responsibility for their decisions.

When a child is punished (spanked):

The spanking or the "giving a talking to" is over quickly and the child's conscience does not develop.

When a child needs to make a choice:

Choice-giving lasts all day. The child continues to think about the choice after it has been given. This helps develop the child's conscience.

If all of the child's life, he is told what to do, when will he learn to make a choice and learn self-responsibility?

• Children learn to live with the consequences of their own choices.

If an adult intervenes, solves the conflict, or punishes the child, what has the child learned?

1. Dad or Mom will stop us if we get out of hand.

2. Instead: We want the children to learn how to make their own choices. Children become self-responsible, self-controlled, and learn impulse control.

Example of Giving a Choice between Two Alternatives

Parent's Goal: To get their eight-year-old daughter to complete her homework by 8:00 p.m.

Parent's Response: "You can choose to complete your homework when you get home from school or right after dinner."

Guidelines for Giving Choices

1. Decide what is most important and work on one choice at a time. Working on several choices at a time can be overwhelming for a child.

2. Give little choices to younger children and bigger choices to older children.

The Oreo Cookie Example: from the video *Choices, Cookies & Kids: A Creative Approach to Discipline* by Garry Landreth

A three-year-old is clutching a large handful of cookies and plans to eat them.

Choice: You may choose to eat one cookie and put the rest back or you may choose to put them all back. Which do you choose?

If the Child Objects:

I know you'd like to have two cookies, but that's not part of the choice. You can *choose* to have one cookie or you can *choose* to put them all back. Which do you *choose*?

If the Child Objects Again:

If you do not *choose*, you *choose* for me to choose. Do you *choose* to have one cookie or do you *choose* to put them all back? (Wait patiently.) I see that you have *chosen* for me to *choose*. I *choose* for you to put all of the cookies back.

PRACTICE: (Giving choices between two alternatives.)

1. Emma has taken a handful of candy. Emma's parents want her to have no more than two pieces of candy.

Emma, you can choose to have _____

or you can choose to have _____

2. After coming home from school, Sarah has sat down in front of the TV with a large bag of chips. Sarah's parents want her to be hungry for dinner in two hours.

Sarah, you can choose to have _____

or you can choose to have _____

When Giving Choices:

When giving choices, it is important for the parent/guardian to communicate no emotion in their voice. Anger or frustration in a parent's voice may indicate the parent is in a power struggle with his child. The child may know how to "wear down" and manipulate the parent in order to get her way.

Some children scream or cry when they are not getting their way. Adults who give in to children when these feelings are expressed are teaching children to scream or cry in order to get their way.

Choices Given as Consequences

(From the video Choices, Cookies & Kids: A Creative Approach to Discipline by Garry Landreth.)

When the Children Did Not Put Away Their Toys:

Issue: The parents are frustrated that their children repeatedly do not put away their toys after playing with them.

Instead of: listening to each child's perspective about what happened, mediating, and attempting to solve the conflict

Get their attention: We are about to institute a new and significant policy and the policy is:

State Two Parts of the Choice:

1. When you *choose* to clean up your toys in the family room, you *choose* to watch your favorite TV show this evening.

2. When you *choose* not to pick up your toys in the family room, you *choose* to not watch your favorite TV show this evening.

Introducing a Choice for the First Time to Children Who Are Fighting in the Car:

1. We are about to institute a new and significant policy and the policy is:

2. When you *choose* not to fight in the back seat of this car, you *choose* to watch TV for this day.

3. When you *choose* to fight, you *choose* to not watch TV for this day.

PRACTICE:

Maggie is responsible for taking out the trash twice a week. Maggie is constantly forgetting to take out the trash.

_____ , when you choose to take out the trash, you choose _____

_____

When you choose not to take out the trash, you choose not to _____

_____

Remember to use both the "positive" as well as the "negative" statement.

Negative Statement Only:

Maggie, when you choose not to take out the trash, you choose not to use the phone for the evening.

Positive and Negative Statements:

Maggie, when you choose to take out the trash, you choose to use the phone for the evening.

When you choose not to take out the trash, you choose not to use the phone for the evening.

Discussion Question:

Why is it important to use both the positive and negative statements?

_____

_____

How is it different than using only the negative statement?

_____

_____

PRACTICE:

When Madison finishes playing, she leaves toys all over the living room floor.

_____ , when you choose to _____

you choose to _____

When you choose not to _____

you choose not to _____

It is a household policy that homework is completed before 8:00 p.m. Mitch, who is ten years old, is playing outside and doesn't begin homework until 7:30 p.m. At 8:00 p.m. one of his favorite TV programs comes on and he has two worksheets left to complete.

_____ , when you _____

_____

When you _____

_____

Gina is responsible for walking the dog every evening before dinner. She frequently forgets. One of Gina's favorite evening activities is to play video games.

_____ , when you _____

_____

When you _____

_____

Dominic is responsible for mowing the lawn during the summer months. He has been asked to mow the lawn on Monday or Tuesday. Frequently the lawn does not get mowed until Thursday or Friday after many verbal reminders. Dominic enjoys swimming in the community pool each afternoon.

_____ , when you _____

_____

When you _____

_____

The Moment You Make a Decision — You Are Committed

Children need to learn that the very moment they make a decision, they are committed.

EXAMPLE: Romano leaves his shoes in the living room.

1. Romano, when you *choose* to put your shoes in your bedroom closet, you *choose* to watch *Sesame Street*.

2. When you *choose* to leave you shoes in the living room, you *choose* not to watch *Sesame Street*.

3. Romano sees his mother coming and runs to pick up the shoes and puts them in the bedroom closet.

4. Romano, I think I know what you have in mind. . . . But the very moment you *chose* to leave your shoes lying on the living room floor, you *chose* not to watch *Sesame Street*.

Discussion Question:

If Romano is able to watch *Sesame Street* after hurrying to get his shoes out of the living room, what is Romano learning?

_____

_____

_____

PRACTICE:

Romano continues to leave clothing and shoes in the living room. His mother wants Romano to begin to put clothing, shoes, and so forth in his bedroom. Provide a choice.

_____ , _____

_____

_____

_____

Romano runs to pick up the things that were left in the living room and plans to take them to the bedroom.

_____ , I think I know what you have in mind. But _____

_____

_____

WRITE YOUR OWN EXAMPLE:

Write an example based upon something that went on at your house when you were a child. Choose something your parents wanted you to become independent and responsible for doing.

Situation: _____

_____

_____

Choice — Positive: _____

_____

Choice — Negative: _____

_____

SPECIAL ISSUES IN PLAY THERAPY

The "Special Issues in Play Therapy" section of this guide describes six different issues for which a child attended play therapy. Excerpts from various play therapy sessions are described with commentary about specific therapeutic responses in the right column.

The "Initial Interaction" section illustrates a series of interactions between the child and play therapist that are in need of improvement. The commentary in the right column describes the therapeutic process and several concerns regarding the quality of the play therapist's therapeutic responses.

The "Corrected Interaction" portion demonstrates effective therapeutic responses and provides commentary that discusses the interaction between the child and therapist. In addition, the commentary describes the rationale for the effectiveness of the therapeutic responses.

CHAPTER 13

CASE STUDY: SCHOOL BEHAVIORAL ISSUE

Four-year-old Mike was brought to play therapy by his mother, Rachel. She reported that the preschool teacher called her numerous times complaining about Mike's disruptive behavior. Rachel recently met with Mike's teacher who informed Rachel that Mike has been throwing toys at other children and calling his classmates derogatory names. Last week, when she confronted Mike, he threw his chair several feet and turned his desk upside down.

Rachel explained to the therapist that she does not have difficulty with Mike at home. She reported that he sometimes challenges rules about snacks and bedtime but that he is generally well behaved. She also described difficulty getting Mike dressed in time to leave for school.

EXCERPT FROM PLAY THERAPY SESSION ONE

Learning Objective — for the play therapist to relax and appropriately follow the child's lead

In the first excerpt, the therapist misses opportunities to follow the child's lead to engage in play when invited. In the corrected section, the therapist follows the child's lead and gains a greater understanding of the child's experience. In addition, the corrected section shows evidence of a stronger relationship between the child and the therapist.

INITIAL INTERACTION

Excerpt #1: In the following excerpt, the therapist does not follow the child's lead to engage in play upon the child's request.

Therapist: Hi Mike. My name is Ms. Harrington. Has your mother talked to you about coming here today?

Therapist introduces herself to Mike.

Mike: Yes, she said I need to get into less trouble in school. She said you are going to help me learn to control myself.

Therapist: This is our playroom and this is a place where you can do a lot of different things.

The therapist introduces the playroom to Mike.

Mike: (Looks around the room quietly.)

Child is uncertain about what is expected. Many children are not use to being given an opportunity to take the lead and to direct their own actions and experiences.

Therapist: I noticed that you're looking around the room at all of the things.

Begin the response with "You're looking around the room at all of the things." Eliminate "I noticed," which places focus on the therapist instead of the child.

Mike: This room is cool. Is all of this for me? (Excitement in his voice.)

Therapist: You're excited about being able to use all these things.

Therapist reflects Mike's feeling of excitement. Reflection of feeling validates Mike and helps him learn to identify and communicate his feelings.

Mike: (Mike walks over to the shelf, picks up two swords, and gives one of the swords to the therapist.) Play swords with me.

Therapist: I choose not to sword fight with you. You can sword fight with the bop bag.

The therapist expressed concern that by engaging in an aggressive activity the child learns that aggression toward another person is acceptable. By not engaging in play with the child, the child may feel rejected and unsure of the therapist.

Mike: (Mike walks over to the bop bag and hits it several times with the sword. Mike looks bored and does not appear angry or aggressive. Mike drops his sword on the ground and walks over to the shelf and picks up a rope.) Here, hold this end and I'll hold the other.

The therapist's concern about not condoning aggression is interfering with her ability to develop a relationship with Mike.

Mike makes another attempt to physically interact with the therapist and build a relationship with the therapist.

Therapist: Okay. I've got this end.	Therapist responds to the child's request verbally (by responding to content) and by holding the end of the rope.
Mike: Now pull real hard. And I'll pull too. Just like tug-of-war. I'm going to pull you on to my side. (Playful tone of voice.)	Child looks forward to the outcome of having the therapist on "his side."
Therapist: I don't like playing tug-of-war. Let's play something that doesn't put us in conflict.	Again, the therapist comments that she felt uncomfortable engaging in play with the child in which they would be in conflict with one another. The therapist uses a word and concept, "conflict," that the child does not understand.
Mike: What is conflict?	Mike needs clarification about what the therapist meant by "conflict."
Therapist: When two people aren't getting along.	Therapist explains the concept of conflict.
Mike: Oh. (Mike walks over to the easel and begins to paint a picture with his back turned toward the therapist.)	Non-verbal behavior clearly indicates that Mike is no longer actively trying to build a relationship with the therapist.
Therapist: You're working hard on your picture.	Therapist acknowledges Mike's efforts. Esteem-building response.
Mike: (Doesn't respond to the therapist's comment.)	Mike tries to connect with the therapist by engaging her in playing swords and tug-of-war. Mike feels rejected by her responses and began playing by himself.

CORRECTED INTERACTION

Excerpt #2: Therapist follows the child's lead, relaxes and engages in play upon the child's request.

Therapist: Hi Mike. My name is Ms. Harrington. Has your mother talked to you about coming here today?

Therapist introduces herself to Mike.

Mike: Yes, she said I need to get into less trouble in school. She said you are going to help me learn to control myself.

Therapist: This is our playroom and this is a place where you can do a lot of different things.

The therapist introduces the playroom to Mike.

Mike: (Looks around the room quietly.)

Child is uncertain about what is expected. Many children are not use to being given an opportunity to take the lead and to direct their own actions and experiences.

Therapist: You're looking around the room at all of the things.

Acknowledging non-verbal behavior.

Mike: This room is cool. Is all of this for me? (Excitement in his voice.)

Therapist: You're excited about being able to use all these things.

Therapist listens to the child's tone of voice and body language to accurately reflect feelings. The therapist reflects Mike's feelings of excitement.

Mike: (Mike walks over to the shelf, picks up two swords and gives one of the swords to the therapist.) Play swords with me.

Therapist: (The therapist holds up the sword and Mike hits his sword against the other sword.) You're working hard at this and you're watching the swords closely.

This response recognizes the child's effort and is a self-esteem building response. The therapist does not focus on feelings of anger or aggression because the child's tone of voice, facial expression, and general body language do not communicate anger or aggression.

Mike: Yeah. I don't want your sword to touch my body. I could get cut. (Mike drops his sword on the ground and walks over to the shelf and picks up a rope.) Here, hold this end and I'll hold the other.

Therapist: Okay. I've got this end.

Therapist communicates to the child that the therapist is following the child's lead.

Mike: Now pull real hard. And I'll pull too. Just like tug-of-war. I'm going to pull you on to my side. (Playful tone of voice.)

Mike's overall affect does not communicate anger or aggression. Mike is looking forward to having the therapist near him "on his side."

Therapist: You want me over there where you are.

Reflection of content acknowledges Mike's intent to have the therapist near him.

Mike: Yeah. Right next to me.

Therapist: (Therapist uses the whisper technique.) What would you like me to do?

The whisper technique keeps the child in the lead.

Mike: Don't pull so hard. Let me pull you over here where I am. (Therapist is now sitting next to Mike.)

The therapist automatically sits next to Mike so that the therapist remains eye level with the child.

Therapist: You wanted me to be a little closer.

Acknowledges Mike's desire to have the therapist closer to him.

Mike: I'm so strong I was able to get you over here right by me.

Child acknowledges his own strengths and abilities.

EXCERPT FROM PLAY THERAPY SESSION TWO

Learning Objective — for the play therapist to reflect feelings

This excerpt shows the significance of identifying and reflecting the child's feelings during the play therapy session. In the first excerpt, the therapist misses many opportunities to respond to Mike's feelings. In the second section, the therapist reflects Mike's feelings and gains a greater understanding of Mike's experience.

INITIAL INTERACTION

Excerpt #1: Therapist missed opportunities to acknowledge the child's feelings.

Introduction to the Session

A few minutes after Mike walked into the play therapy room he got down on his hands and knees and began to crawl around the room. He announced that he was a cat and began to meow.

Mike: Meow. Meow. I'm a cat. I don't have a home. (Mike crawls next to the therapist. Mike's tone of voice sounds sad.)

Therapist: You're pretending to be a cat without a home.

Therapist misses the opportunity to respond to Mike's feeling of sadness. Therapist needs to observe facial expression, body gestures, and tone of voice in order to respond to child's affect.

Mike: (Child crawls next to therapist's leg and begins scratching the wall.) I am. I have no family. Meow. Meow. (Pretends to lick a plastic ball. Voice still sounds sad.)

Therapist: You like being a cat.	The therapist responds to the fact that the child is enjoying the role of being a cat. Therapist misses the opportunity to respond to the child's sadness and the significant message that the cat has "no family."
Mike: I'm done being a cat. I'm going to paint a picture.	Child disengages in this metaphorical play and decides to engage in a different activity.
Therapist: You're finished being a cat.	Reflects content but misses the overall message that the child does not feel understood.

CORRECTED INTERACTION

Excerpt #2: Therapist reflects the child's feelings.

Mike: Meow. Meow. I'm a cat. I don't have a home. (Mike crawled next to the therapist. Mike's tone of voice sounded sad.)	
Therapist: You sound so very sad.	Therapist recognizes the sadness in the child's tone of voice and acknowledges the sadness. Therapist reflects feeling.
Mike: (Child crawls next to therapist's leg and begins scratching the wall.) I am. I have no family. I'm from a one-person family.	Note that the reflection of feeling results in child explaining reason for feeling sad.
Therapist: You feel lonely and want someone to be with you.	Therapist anticipates feeling of loneliness and reflects feeling.
Mike: I know. I can take care of myself. (Mike crawls over to the baby bed, gets inside and covers himself with a blanket.)	Reflection of feelings facilitates child's expressing new behaviors.

Therapist: Since you can't find anyone to care for you right now, you decided to take care of yourself. You found a bed to lie down in and a soft blanket.	Therapist acknowledged the child's content, non-verbal actions, and coping skills.
Mike: Yes, I'm tired and need some rest.	Child feels understood.

EXCERPT FROM PLAY THERAPY SESSION SIX

Learning Objective — for the play therapist to identify and respond to opportunities to reflect the child's feelings

This excerpt also illustrates the significance of acknowledging and validating children's feelings during the play therapy session. By reflecting feelings, the therapist deepens the session and learns more about Mike and Mike's experience. This interchange between the child and therapist shows how the direction of the play session could change if the therapist continues to miss opportunities to reflect Mike's feelings or the doll's feelings.

INITIAL INTERACTION

Excerpt #1: Therapist missed opportunities to reflect the child's feelings.

Introduction to the Session

Mike enters the playroom and looks around at the various toys and play materials. He walks over to the shelf and focuses his attention on two G.I. Joe - type male dolls.

Mike: This doll is ugly. It has dark hair. (Looks at the doll with an expression of disgust and throws it aside. Reaches for another doll.) This doll is smart and strong. It has light hair. This one is much better.	
Therapist: One is ugly and one is smart and strong.	Therapist describes characteristics of both dolls but does not acknowledge Mike's like or dislike for either doll.

Mike: Yeah, the other one is ugly. (Mike picks up the doll with dark hair, walks over to the sandbox and slowly starts to bury it. Mike begins to speak as the doll's voice.) I'm being buried deep down, far and deep down. (Voice tone sounds sad.)

Therapist: You are burying the doll deep into the sand.

Therapist missed the opportunity to acknowledge the doll's sadness. At this point the direction of therapy changes.

Mike: Yep. I don't want to see it. (Finishes burying the doll.)

Therapist: You want it hidden.

Therapist acknowledges content of Mike's communication. Therapist missed the opportunity to acknowledge that Mike did not like the doll he was burying.

Mike: (Reaches to get the doll with light hair. Holds the doll upright on top of the sand's surface and speaks for the doll.) I am happy and strong. I am the best!

Therapist: (Speaks directly to the doll.) You really like yourself.

Therapist uses an esteem-building response with the doll and acknowledges the doll's positive feelings toward himself.

Mike: I am the best! I am the best!

Therapist: Hmm.

CORRECTED INTERACTION

Excerpt #2: Therapist reflects the child's feelings

Mike: This doll is ugly. It has dark hair. (Looks at the doll with an expression of disgust and throws it aside. Reaches for another doll.) This doll is smart and strong. It has light hair. This one is much better.

Therapist: You like the strong doll with light hair more than the other one.

Therapist reflects feeling and content.

Mike: Yeah, the other one is ugly. (Mike picks up the doll with dark hair, walks over to the sandbox and slowly starts to bury it. Mike begins to speak as the doll's voice.) I'm being buried deep down, far and deep down. (Voice tone sounds sad.)

Therapist: You sound so very sad. (In a somber voice.)

Therapist matches Mike's sadness in his tone of voice and reflects Mike's feelings of sadness.

Mike: I am . . . I am dying. I don't know what to do. (Finishes burying the doll.)

Therapist: You feel helpless and sad. You're dying. (In a quiet and sad tone of voice.)

Reflecting feelings can be a challenge for some beginning therapists. The therapist responds to the child's affective state by reflecting feeling and content in a quiet and sad tone of voice.

Mike: (Reaches to get the doll with light hair. Holds the doll upright on top of the sand's surface and speaks for the doll.) I am happy and strong. I can do lots of things. I hate the doll with dark hair. That doll is bad . . . very bad.

Therapist: You really like the strong and happy doll. You hate the other one and think it is bad.

Therapist reflects the child's like and dislike for each doll.

Mike: It is bad. It never does anything right.

Note that the previous reflection of feeling results in the child explaining his reason for thinking the doll is bad.

Therapist: You get angry at it for making so many mistakes.

Therapist reflects feeling of anger and content.

Mike: Well, it just makes too many mistakes. No one likes him. He's bad.

Note that the reflection of feeling results in further explanation by the child that "no one likes" the doll.

Therapist: He must be so lonely and feel so sad that no one likes him.

Therapist anticipates the doll's feeling of sadness and loneliness and reflects these feelings.

Mike: He just needs to be more like the light-haired doll and then he'd have more friends.

CHAPTER 14

CASE STUDY: GRIEF LOSS

Five-year-old Kaleigh was brought to play therapy by her mother, Michelle. Michelle reported that Kaleigh is not sleeping through the night since her four month-old sister, Elissa, died of SIDS six weeks ago. She also explained that Kaleigh's appetite has dramatically decreased and that she visits the school nurse's office on a daily basis complaining of stomachaches. Kaleigh's teacher reported that in the last six weeks Kaleigh becomes easily angered and will not follow simple instructions such as moving from her desk to the story circle. Her teacher reported that Kaleigh will crawl under her desk, curl up in a ball, and ignore the teacher several times a day.

Michelle stated that she and her spouse had noticed changes in Kaleigh's behavior but had hoped that with time Kaleigh would return to her typical behavior.

EXCERPT FROM PLAY THERAPY SESSION ONE

Learning Objective — to identify opportunities to facilitate encouragement and esteem-building and to reflect feeling and content

In the initial interaction, the therapist misses opportunities to facilitate encouragement and esteem-building and misses opportunities to reflect feeling and content. In the corrected interaction, the therapist acknowledges the child's non-verbal behavior and reflects feeling and content when the opportunity is presented.

INITIAL INTERACTION

Excerpt #1: In the following excerpt, the therapist misses opportunities to facilitate encouragement and esteem-building and misses opportunities to reflect feeling and content. (Dialogue begins five minutes into the session.)

Kaleigh: (Kaleigh has been trying to open the play handcuffs for several minutes.) Why won't these things open?

Therapist: You're wondering why they won't open.

Therapist responds to Kaleigh's content but misses the opportunity to acknowledge Kaleigh's frustration and an opportunity to acknowledge her efforts and persistence.

Kaleigh: That's what I want to know. Why won't these dumb things open? (Kaleigh throws the handcuffs on the floor.)

Therapist: You decided to play with something else.

Therapist makes a response to acknowledge Kaleigh's decision-making ability but misses an opportunity to reflect feelings of anger and frustration.

Kaleigh: Yeah, they won't work for me.

Therapist: You're figuring out what you want to do next.

The therapist's response encourages Kaleigh to continue taking the lead and determining the direction of the session.

Kaleigh: (Walks over to the baby doll, picks up the baby doll, and throws it down on the floor.) I killed it. (In a sad voice.)

General body language, including the throwing action, seems filled with anger. However, the tone of voice indicates sadness. This may be indicative of the child's grieving process and feelings of anger and sadness over the loss.

Therapist: Wow.

Therapist misses the opportunity to reflect Kaleigh's feelings and content. (During supervision, the therapist stated that she was shocked and was uncertain what to say to Kaleigh.)

Kaleigh: (Walks over to the easel and begins to paint.)

Kaleigh quickly changed the activity from throwing the doll on the floor to painting at the easel. This play disruption may indicate that Kaleigh's feelings are so intense that Kaleigh needs a break from the issue or activity.

Therapist: You have a plan. You really want to paint.	Therapist acknowledges Kaleigh's initiative and decision to engage in another activity. This response facilitates decision-making.
Kaleigh: (Begins painting a large yellow sun in the center of her paper. Paints eyes and a smile on the sun.)	
Therapist: You painted a happy face on the sun.	Therapist acknowledges Kaleigh's actions.
Kaleigh: It's not happy at all. (Quickly covers the sun with black paint.)	Kaleigh's comment indicates that she does not feel that her intentions were understood.
Therapist: You changed your mind. You decided not to make it happy.	Therapist verbally acknowledges Kaleigh's feedback and uses a response that acknowledges her decision-making ability.
Kaleigh: It wasn't ever going to be happy. (Irritated tone of voice.)	Kaleigh still feels misunderstood and tries to communicate her intent to the therapist a second time.
Therapist: Oh.	Therapist misses an opportunity to acknowledge Kaleigh's irritation and intent. (During supervision, therapist stated she was surprised by the intensity of the irritation in Kaleigh's voice.)
Kaleigh: I said — the sun wasn't ever going to be happy! (Angry tone of voice.)	Kaleigh expresses feelings of anger over not having her most recent comment "it wasn't ever going to be happy" acknowledged.
Therapist: Okay.	The therapist misses an opportunity to validate Kaleigh's feelings and correct her inaccurate response about the happy face on the sun.

CORRECTED INTERACTION

Excerpt #2: Therapist reflects feeling and content and looks for opportunities to facilitate esteem building.

Kaleigh: (Kaleigh has been trying to open the play handcuffs for several minutes.) Why won't these things open? (Irritation in tone of voice.)

Therapist: Even though you're very frustrated that you can't get them open, you keep trying to figure out different ways to open them.

The therapist acknowledges Kaleigh's feeling of frustration and her efforts and persistence. "You keep trying to figure out different ways to open them" is an esteem-building response that acknowledges Kaleigh's efforts and persistence. Acknowledging a child's effort provides the child with feedback that can be internalized. On the other hand, general praise such as "good job" does not describe the effort needed to accomplish a task. The child is unable to internalize the message "good job" since it is another individual's opinion and not based on descriptive, factual information. This type of praise teaches the child to look to others (external sources) to feel good about oneself.

Kaleigh: I'm going to figure this out soon. There it is! They are open.

Therapist: You're excited that all your hard work paid off.

Therapist acknowledges Kaleigh's excitement that she was capable of opening the handcuffs.

Kaleigh: (Kaleigh's mood shifts to quiet and somber as she puts the handcuffs on herself.) I'm going to jail.

Therapist: You're going to jail and you sound so sad.

Therapist notices a change in Kaleigh's body language and tone of voice. Therapist acknowledges Kaleigh's sadness and the fact that she is going to jail.

Kaleigh: Everything is sad these days.

Therapist: You're so sad that it's hard to find anything to be happy about.

Therapist acknowledges how overwhelming Kaleigh's feelings of sadness are.

Kaleigh: (Takes off the handcuffs, walks over and picks up the baby doll and throws it down on the floor.) I killed it. (In a sad voice.)

Therapist: You think you killed the baby and you're very, very sad.

Therapist acknowledges Kaleigh's sadness and that Kaleigh feels responsible for killing the baby.

Kaleigh: I did kill the baby. I killed Elissa and I should be taken to jail. (Looks down at the baby doll on the floor.)

Kaleigh mentions Elissa's name and her feelings and concerns become directly related to her and the death of her sister Elissa.

Therapist: You think you're to blame for Elissa's death.

The therapist acknowledges the content of Kaleigh's message.

Kaleigh: I am. When she came home from the hospital with Mom, it seemed that Mom didn't love me anymore. I made a wish that Elissa would die. (Tone of voice sounds angry and sad.)

As a result of the therapist's reflection, the child explains why she thinks she is to blame for Elissa's death.

Therapist: You are so sad and angry at yourself. You think that your wish killed Elissa. You really needed to know that your mother still loved you too.

Therapist acknowledges Kaleigh's feelings of sadness and anger and the content that she thinks that her wish killed Elissa. The therapist anticipated that she knew Kaleigh's need to know that her mother still loved her.

Kaleigh: Yes. I didn't really want Elissa to die. (Bends down and picks up the baby doll and holds it close.) I wish she was alive.

EXCERPT FROM SESSION TWO

Learning Objective — to learn how to use the whisper technique to keep the child in the lead

This excerpt focuses on the importance of utilizing the whisper technique when the child asks the therapist to join in the play. The whisper technique creates the opportunity for the child to continue leading the therapeutic play process and determine the direction of therapy.

The whisper technique is frequently used when the child invites the therapist to be a part of the child's play. When the child asks the therapist to play, the therapist uses a whisper tone of voice, and asks the child "what would you like me to do" or "what would you like me to say?" This returns the responsibility for the direction of the therapeutic play to the child.

This excerpt shows an example of how a therapist joined in the child's play process. In the initial interaction, the therapist does not use the whisper technique and guesses how the child wants him to participate in the play. This process takes the play in a direction determined by the therapist and the child is no longer leading the play or the therapeutic process. As a result, the therapist determines the direction for therapy.

In the corrected interaction, the child invites the therapist to join in her play and the therapist uses the whisper technique to join in the child's play while providing the child an opportunity to continue leading the direction of the therapeutic process.

INITIAL INTERACTION

Excerpt #1: The therapist joins in the child's play but does not use the whisper technique.

Introduction to the Session

After being in the playroom about ten minutes, Kaleigh begins playing with the dollhouse and the doll family. She looks at the therapist and asks the therapist to play dollhouse with her.

Kaleigh: I want you to play doll family with me.

Therapist: Okay. (Therapist walks over to the dollhouse and sits down near Kaleigh.)	Therapist acknowledges Kaleigh's request that the therapist play dolls with her.

Kaleigh: This is the mommy and this is the daddy. Here is the big sister and this is the baby.

Therapist: I'll be the daddy and the baby.

Therapist begins leading the process by telling Kaleigh which dolls he wants to be.

Kaleigh: (Sighs) Okay. I'll be the big sister and the mommy.

Therapist: You sounded disappointed. Do you want to be someone different?

Therapist recognizes child's disappointment and reflects this feeling.

Kaleigh: No, no, this is okay.

The therapist uses the "daddy doll" and the child uses the "big sister doll" during the following interactions.

Therapist: (Therapist walks the daddy doll toward the big sister.) What's wrong?

Kaleigh: Nothing.

Therapist: Oh, okay. Are you sure? What's wrong?

Therapist notices something is wrong and asks for feedback. Child wants to use different dolls but doesn't feel comfortable asking the therapist to change dolls.

Kaleigh: I don't know.

Therapist: You're not sure what's really wrong.

Acknowledges child's uncertainty.

Kaleigh: Yeah.

Therapist: (Holds the baby doll in front of Kaleigh's big sister doll.) Do you like me?

Therapist asks the doll (child) a question. This question continues to put the therapist in the lead and the therapist is determining the direction of therapy.

Kaleigh: Yeah. I like you.

Therapist: So, you really like me.	The therapist reflects and acknowledges the child's content.
Kaleigh: Well sometimes. Mommy is always taking care of you.	The previous reflection invites the child to explain further.
Therapist: That's because I'm little.	The therapist does not use the whisper technique and takes this opportunity to explain why the mother needs to take care of her younger sibling.
Kaleigh: Well, hurry up and grow up! I'm tired of you being little.	
Therapist: I want you to like me.	The therapist's response leads the therapy session in a direction determined by the therapist. The child is not provided an opportunity to explore her concerns, feelings, or experiences. Instead, she automatically responds to the therapist's comments and responses.
Kaleigh: Well I don't, okay. Go away.	
Therapist: You wish I would just disappear.	Therapist acknowledges content of the child's communication.
Kaleigh: Yes! Go away! (Anger in tone of voice.)	
Therapist: You sound really angry at me.	Therapist responds to anger in child's tone of voice and reflects anger feeling.
Kaleigh: I am. Now go away!	
Therapist: You're very angry.	

CORRECTED INTERACTION

Excerpt #2: Therapist joins in the child's play and uses the whisper technique to provide the opportunity to lead the therapeutic process.

Kaleigh: I want you to play doll family with me.

Therapist: Okay. (Therapist walks over to the dollhouse and sits down near Kaleigh.)

Therapist acknowledges Kaleigh's request verbally and by walking toward Kaleigh and the dollhouse.

Kaleigh: This is the mommy and this is the daddy. Here is the big sister and this is the baby.

Therapist: You're introducing everyone in the family.

Therapist reflects Kaleigh's content.

Kaleigh: Yeah. Who do you want to be?

Therapist: (Using a whisper voice.) Who would you like me to be?

Therapist uses the whisper technique to find out what Kaleigh wants his role to be in the family.

Kaleigh: I want you to be the mommy and the baby and I will be the daddy and the big sister. (Looks up at the therapist.)

Therapist: (Using a whisper voice.) What would you like me to do?

Therapist uses the whisper technique to provide Kaleigh the opportunity to create the story and the direction of the therapeutic process.

Kaleigh: I want you to be the mommy and to tell the big sister how much you love her.

Therapist: (Therapist walks the mother doll over to the big sister doll.) I want you to know how much I love you and how precious you are to me.

Therapist responds using the feedback and request Kaleigh made in her most recent response.

Kaleigh: If you love me, why don't you have time for me anymore?

Therapist: (Using a whisper voice.) What do you want me to say?

Therapist uses the whisper technique to find out how Kaleigh wants the therapeutic process to proceed.

Kaleigh: Tell her the baby takes a lot of time but that you still really love her as much as the baby.

Therapist: (Uses the mother doll to respond.) The baby needs a lot of attention.

Therapist begins to respond to Kaleigh's request.

Kaleigh: (Kaleigh interrupts the therapist in an angry tone of voice.) I don't care. Sometimes I hate the baby. I want things to be the way they used to be.

Therapist: (Uses the mother doll to respond.) You're angry and sad that we don't have more time to spend together. You wish it could be just you and me again so I could give you more attention and love.

The therapist did not have to use the whisper technique to follow the child's lead. The therapist has the "mother" doll respond to the feelings and content of Kaleigh's response. This still keeps Kaleigh in the lead and responds to her feelings and concerns.

Kaleigh: Yeah. Why did you have to have another baby? (Angry tone of voice.)

Therapist: Sometimes you really feel angry at the baby for taking time away from us.

The therapist has the "mother" doll respond to Kaleigh's feelings. The therapist continues to respond to Kaleigh's feelings and concerns.

Kaleigh: I wish it were dead!

Therapist: You feel so angry that you wish the baby was dead.

The therapist uses the "mother" doll to respond to the feelings and content of Kaleigh's message. The therapist does not judge or discount Kaleigh's statement by making a comment such as "you don't really wish the baby was dead." This type of response communicates to the child that the comment was inappropriate and should not have been made. As a result, the child may refrain from communicating other feelings and thoughts to the therapist.

Kaleigh: Yeah but not really dead. I just miss you, Mommy. Do you still love me?

Therapist: (whisper technique) What would you like me to say?

Beginning therapists may want to reassure Kaleigh by responding with a message of love and deep appreciation. Instead, the therapist uses the whisper technique to make certain that the therapist is responding to the feelings and concerns the child expresses.

Kaleigh: Tell me how much you love me and how special I am. And, tell me you want to spend more time together.

Therapist: You wish I could spend more time with you. I love you very much. No one can ever replace you. You are very special to me.

Therapist uses the "mother" doll to respond to Kaleigh's concern about being loved by her mother.

Kaleigh: (Looks up at the therapist and smiles.)

Therapist: You like what the mommy just said to the big sister. It feels good to know how special you are and how much you're really loved.

Therapist acknowledges Kaleigh's smile that was made in response to the last comment made by the "mother" doll.

Kaleigh: (Gently holding the baby doll figure, sad tone of voice.) I wished her to be alive and she isn't alive. My wish didn't come true.

Therapist: You are so sad that you're sister has died. You wish she could be alive again.

Kaleigh: I can't wish her alive and I really couldn't make her die from a wish. That's what Daddy told me and I really think he's right.

Therapist acknowledges Kaleigh's thoughts and feelings.

CHAPTER 15

CASE STUDY: SIBLING RIVALRY

Five-year-old Kendra and seven-year-old Tamara were brought to play therapy by their mother, Kashana. Kashana reported that Kendra and Tamara had minimal conflicts in the past. However, ever since she and their biological father separated four months ago, the conflicts have increased. Kashana explained that the girls are scratching and punching each other. She stated that they frequently pull one another's hair, slam the bedroom door, and throw clothes and shoes at one another. Kashana stated that it seems that the girls are constantly yelling, name calling, and physically fighting from the time they get home from school until bedtime.

Kashana stated that Tamara, the seven-year-old, should know better than to fight with her five-year-old sister. Kashana reported that Kendra, the five-year-old, frequently runs to her crying and complaining that Tamara has been mean to her or has hit her. Kashana explained to the therapist that she has tried time out, taking away privileges, and grounding Tamara but that no form of discipline seems to help diminish the constant conflict.

Sibling and Group Play Therapy

When facilitating a group play therapy session, one of the most challenging communication issues for beginning play therapists is to address each child individually.

The following example illustrates this issue.

INITIAL INTERACTION

Tamara: (Gives a toy to her younger sister Kendra.) Here, Kendra.

Therapist: Kendra, you look happy to get that toy from her.

CORRECTED INTERACTION

Tamara: (Gives a toy to her younger sister Kendra.) Here, Kendra.

Therapist: Tamara, you wanted to share that toy with Kendra. And, Kendra, you look happy that Tamara is sharing that toy with you.

EXCERPT FROM PLAY THERAPY SESSION THREE

Learning Objective — for the therapist to learn to address the concerns of each individual child and to use the ACT limit-setting model.

INITIAL INTERACTION

Excerpt #1: In the following excerpt, the therapist misses opportunities to respond to each child's feelings and concerns and the therapist does not use the ACT limit-setting model.

(Dialogue begins approximately ten minutes into the session.)

Kendra: (Opens the doctor's kit and asks Tamara a question.) Can I look in your ear?

Tamara: Okay.

Kendra: (Looks in Tamara's ear.)

Tamara: Stop, that hurts! You're pressing too hard.

Therapist: You want her to stop. (Kendra continues looking in Tamara's ear.)	Therapist responds to Tamara's message or content.
Tamara: Stop, I said! (Angrily grabs the toy out of Kendra's hand and throws it on the floor.)	
Therapist: You're angry that Kendra didn't stop.	Therapist acknowledges Tamara's feeling and content. The therapist also needed to acknowledge Kendra by stating "when Tamara asked you to stop looking in her ear, you did not want to stop."
Kendra: (Begins shooting therapist with the plastic gun.)	Kendra expresses anger toward the therapist by aiming a plastic dart gun at the therapist.

Therapist: You were angry at Tamara and now you're angry at me too.	Therapist reflects Kendra's feeling of anger toward Tamara and the therapist.
Kendra: (Loads the plastic gun with a plastic dart and aims it at the therapist.)	Review of the ACT limit-setting model proposed by Landreth (2002). The ACT model is most effective when all three parts of the limit-setting model are used. 1. A — the therapist acknowledges the child's feelings, which communicates acknowledgment and acceptance of feelings 2. C — the therapist communicates the limit in a calm, nonjudgmental manner 3. T — the therapist targets an acceptable alternative
Therapist: Kendra, I'm not for shooting.	Therapist uses one part of the ACT limit-setting model. The therapist only communicates the limit and does not acknowledge Kendra's feelings or target an alternate behavior.
Kendra: I can shoot you if I want to.	
Therapist: Kendra, I'm not for shooting. You can shoot something else.	The therapist again communicates the limit (C) and provides a vague alternative (T). The therapist still needs to acknowledge Kendra's feelings (A) and provide a specific alternate behavior (T).
Kendra: Okay! I'll shoot Tamara.	
Tamara: Kendra, I can't stand you. You're such a baby.	The therapist does not respond to Tamara's statement labeling Kendra a baby. Kendra may perceive that the therapist is siding with Tamara.
Therapist: Kendra, people aren't for shooting, you can shoot the bop bag.	The therapist communicates the limit (C) and targets a specific alternate behavior for expressing her anger (T).

	However, the therapist does not acknowledge Kendra's feelings first (A).
	Acknowledging the child's feeling first (A), helps the child feel understood and more likely to listen to the remaining part of the ACT limit-setting response.
Kendra: I'm not a baby. Aims the plastic dart gun at Tamara. (Angry tone of voice.)	Kendra's tone of voice expresses anger that Tamara called her a "baby."
Therapist: Kendra, Tamara is not for shooting. You can shoot the bop bag.	The therapist does not respond to Kendra's anger or address the fact the Tamara called Kendra a baby.
Kendra: I don't want to shoot the bop bag. I want to shoot Tamara. I hate her!	
Therapist: Kendra, even though you're angry Tamara is not for shooting.	The therapist used two parts of the ACT model. The therapist (A) acknowledges Kendra's anger and (C) communicates a limit. The therapist did not (T) target an alternate behavior.
Kendra: I don't care. I'll shoot her anyway. (Shoots a plastic dart at Tamara.)	

CORRECTED INTERACTION

Excerpt #2: Therapist reflects the concerns and experiences of each child and sets limits using the ACT limit-setting model.

Kendra: (Opens the doctor's kit and asks Tamara a question.)
Can I look in your ear?

Tamara: Okay.

Kendra: (Looks in Tamara's ear.)

Tamara: Stop, that hurts! You're pressing too hard.

Therapist: You want Kendra to stop looking in your ear. (Kendra continues looking in Tamara's ear.)

Therapist acknowledges Tamara's concern and the content of her statement.

Tamara: Stop, I said! (Angrily grabs the toy out of Kendra's hand and throws it on the floor.)

Therapist: Tamara, you're angry that Kendra didn't stop and Kendra you wanted to keep on looking.

Therapist acknowledges the feelings and concerns of each child.

Tamara: Kendra, I hate when you don't listen. I hate it!

Therapist: Tamara, you get angry when Kendra doesn't listen to what's important to you.

Therapist reflects Tamara's anger about not being listened to by her sister Kendra.

Kendra: (Picks up the stethoscope.)
Can I listen to your heart Tamara?

Tamara: No! Leave me alone. I don't want to play with you right now!

Kendra: You're a baby, a big baby. You don't have a heart.

Therapist: Tamara, you're angry right now and you don't want to play with Kendra. Kendra, you're angry that Tamara doesn't want to play with you.

Therapist reflects Tamara's and Kendra's feelings of anger in two separate statements. The therapist wants to communicate understanding to each child.

Kendra: Yeah. Tell her that she has to play with me.

Therapist: Kendra, you wish I could make her play with you; but right now, Tamara, you choose not to play with Kendra.

Therapist is careful to acknowledge both children. Acknowledging only one child may be perceived as rejection by the child who was not acknowledged. Therapist addresses Kendra's concerns while also acknowledging Tamara's desire not to play with Kendra.

Kendra: (Picks up the plastic snake from the shelf, walks over to the therapist and throws it onto the therapist and laughs loudly.)

Therapist: Kendra, you're angry that I didn't tell Tamara to play with you. But I'm not for throwing at. You can tell me with words "I'm angry at you."

Therapist acknowledges Kendra's anger that the therapist did not instruct Tamara to play with Kendra as Kendra requested. The therapist uses the ACT limit-setting model described below.

Kendra: (Picks up the plastic knife and acts like she is cutting the therapist's arm and laughs.)

Kendra does not respond to targeted behavior described by the therapist. Instead, she chooses another activity to show her anger toward the therapist.

Therapist: Kendra, you're very angry at me but I'm not for cutting. You can pretend the bop bag is me and cut the bop bag instead.

Therapist uses the ACT model proposed by Landreth (2002).
1. A — the therapist acknowledges Kendra's feelings which communicates acknowledgment and acceptance of her feelings ("You're very angry at me").
2. C — the therapist communicates the limit in a calm, nonjudgmental manner ("I'm not for cutting").
3. T — the therapist targets an acceptable alternative ("You can

147

pretend the bop bag is me and cut the bop bag instead").

Since the targeted alternate behavior (using the statement "I'm angry at you") did not work during the previous limit-setting, the therapist chose an alternate behavior that would provide an opportunity for a physical release of the anger.

Kendra: (Walks over to the bop bag and runs the plastic knife across it several times.) The girls continue to engage in several more conflicts throughout the session.

EXCERPT FROM PLAY THERAPY SESSION EIGHT

INITIAL INTERACTION

Excerpt #1: In the following excerpt, the therapist misses opportunities to respond to each child's feelings and concerns and the therapist does not use the ACT limit-setting model.

(Dialogue begins twenty minutes into the session.)

Tamara: (Bumps her elbow on the edge of the puppet theater and begins to cry loudly and yell.) It hurts! It hurts! (Tone of voice is sad and angry.)	The therapist misses an opportunity to respond to Tamara's feelings of pain and anger.
Kendra: Hurry! Call 9-1-1! (Picks up the toy phone.) Is this 9-1-1? Hurry up. Come and help my sister. She is really hurt! (Looks at Tamara.) They are coming!	
Tamara: (Continues to cry loudly.) It still hurts!	Therapist misses an opportunity to respond to Tamara's hurt.
Kendra: (Gets the medical kit. Makes a noise like an ambulance siren.) They are here! Here, let me help you, ma'am. Do you need some medicine?	
Tamara: I don't want medicine. Get away from me. (Tone of voice—frustrated.)	Therapist misses an opportunity to reflect Tamara's feelings.
Kendra: (Puts medicine bottle near Tamara's mouth.)	Therapist does not acknowledge Kendra's desire to help Tamara.
Tamara: Get away from me! (Anger.)	The therapist did not respond to Tamara's feeling of anger.
Kendra: (Kendra angrily pushes Tamara and walks away.)	
Therapist: People aren't for pushing. You can tell Tamara "I'm angry at you."	The therapist does not acknowledge Kendra's anger toward Tamara. Therapist does not use the (A) part of the ACT limit-setting model before using the (C) and (T) responses.

Kendra: I am angry at you!	The therapist misses an opportunity to respond to Kendra's feeling of anger.
Tamara: (Looks at therapist.) She can't make my pain go away.	
Therapist: Oh.	The therapist misses an opportunity to respond to Tamara's pain.
Tamara: My elbow is feeling a little better. I'll put some water on it. (Wets a paper towel and places it on her elbow.)	
Kendra: It's so nice that she quit crying.	The therapist misses an opportunity to respond to Kendra's content and feeling of relief.
Tamara: (Throws the wet paper towel into the trash can and walks over to the suitcase. Tamara begins putting clothing into the suitcase.) I'm packing up and leaving. I'm moving to another house. This house is dirty and it will never get cleaned up. (Sounds angry and disgusted.)	During group play therapy, verbal and physical interaction between the children occurs quickly. It can be challenging for beginning play therapists to interject responses that acknowledge the children's feelings, content, and experience.
Kendra: I want to come with you. You can't leave without me. (Begins throwing clothing into the suitcase.)	
Tamara: Okay. You can come too.	
Tamara: Yeah. This house is old and dirty. It can't be cleaned it's so dirty. It's time to move somewhere else.	The therapist misses opportunities to acknowledge the children's feelings, content, and experience.
Kendra: (Looks at Tamara.) Where are we going?	
Tamara: To the other side of town. There is a nice, new house there we can live in. Get in the car. Come on, let's go. (Makes the noise of a car driving fast.)	

Kendra: Are we there yet?

Tamara: Here we are! Look at this place. It is new and clean. I'm glad we left that dirty old place. (Tone of voice is happy and relieved.)

Therapist: You both arrived at the new house.

Therapist acknowledges the content of Tamara's message but did not respond to her feelings.

Kendra: Our parents are getting a divorce you know. We have to do a lot of moving.

CORRECTED INTERACTION

Excerpt #2: Therapist reflects the concerns and experiences of each child and sets limits using the ACT limit-setting model.

Tamara: (Bumps her elbow on the edge of the puppet theater and begins to cry loudly and yell.) It hurts! It hurts! (Tone of voice is sad and angry.)

Therapist: You're in a lot of pain and you're angry that you hurt your elbow.

The therapist responds to Tamara's feelings of hurt and anger.

Kendra: Hurry! Call 9-1-1! (Picks up the toy phone.) Is this 9-1-1? Hurry up. Come and help my sister. She is really hurt! (Looks at Tamara.) They are coming!

Tamara: (Continues to cry loudly.) It still hurts!

Therapist: The hurt hasn't gone away.

Therapist responds to Tamara's feeling and content.

Kendra: (Gets the medical kit. Makes a noise like an ambulance siren.) They are here! Here, let me help you, ma'am. Do you need some medicine?

Tamara: (Kendra offers a plastic medicine bottle to Tamara.) I don't want medicine. Get away from me.

Therapist: Kendra, you want to help Tamara and Tamara you don't want Kendra's help right now.

The therapist acknowledges each child's individual experience and concerns.

Kendra: (Kendra angrily pushes Tamara and walks away.)

Therapist: Kendra, you're angry at Tamara for not letting you help. People aren't for pushing. You can tell Tamara "I'm angry at you."

Therapist uses the ACT limit-setting model.

Kendra: I am angry at you!

Kendra decides to use the targeted alternate behavior and tells Tamara that she is angry at her.

Tamara: (Looks at therapist.) She can't make my pain go away.

Tamara looks to the therapist for understanding.

Therapist: It still hurts a lot.

The therapist responds to the hurt that Tamara is experiencing.

Tamara: My elbow is feeling a little better. I'll put some water on it. (Wets a paper towel and places it on her elbow.)

Therapist: You figured out a way to help yourself.

The therapist acknowledges that Tamara figured out a way to help herself. (Self-responsibility response.)

Tamara: (Throws the wet paper towel into the trash can and walks over to the suitcase. Tamara begins putting clothing into the suitcase.) I'm packing up and leaving. I'm moving to another house. This house is dirty and it will never get cleaned up. (Sounds angry and disgusted.)

Therapist: You're so angry you want to live in a different home . . . a home that isn't so dirty.

Therapist acknowledges Tamara's anger and desire to live in a cleaner home.

Kendra: I want to come with you. You can't leave without me. (Begins throwing clothing into the suitcase.)

Tamara: Okay. You can come too.

Therapist: Kendra, it's important to you to be with your sister and Tamara you agreed to have Kendra come with you.

Therapist responds to Kendra and Tamara's individual responses and collective plan to pack their belongings and move into another house.

Tamara: Yeah. This house is old and falling down. It can't be cleaned it's so dirty. It's time to move somewhere else.

Therapist: You want to move. The house is so old that it is falling down.

The therapist acknowledges the content of Tamara's response.

Kendra: (Looks at Tamara.) Where are we going?

Tamara: To the other side of town. There is a nice, new house there we can live in. Get in the car. Come on, let's go. (Makes the noise of a car driving fast.)

Kendra: Are we there yet?

Tamara: Here we are! Look at this place. It is new and clean. I'm glad we left that dirty old place. (Tone of voice is happy and relieved.)

Therapist: You sound happy to be in your new house.

Therapist responds to Tamara's feelings of relief and happiness.

Tamara: I sure am!

Kendra: Our parents are getting a divorce you know. We have to move.

CHAPTER 16

CASE STUDY: ANGER AND AGGRESSION

Jason, a five-year-old male, was referred to counseling due to domestic violence in the home. Jason's mother reported that Jason had witnessed violence between her and his father. Jason's mother stated that Jason had difficulty following directions and often had "temper tantrums" when he did not get his way. She further reported that Jason was often remorseful after his temper tantrums. Although there was domestic violence in the home, both parents were receiving services at the time and were still living in the same house.

In the therapeutic setting, Jason was often slow to enter the playroom and expressed anger toward any limits set in the playroom. Jason was also openly angry and aggressive toward the therapist during the sessions. Following is an excerpt of a beginning session with Jason.

EXCERPT FROM PLAY THERAPY SESSION ONE

Learning Objective — for the play therapist to reflect the child's feelings and integrate the use of different types of therapeutic responses

In the first excerpt, the therapist does not acknowledge the child's feelings and does not use appropriate limit-setting techniques. In the corrected section, the therapist responds to the child's feelings and uses the ACT limit-setting model. The corrected section also demonstrates how the use of therapeutic responses can impact the direction of a session.

INITIAL INTERACTION

Excerpt #1: In the following excerpt, the therapist does not reflect the child's feelings and does not use the ACT limit-setting model.

Jason: (With arms folded and head down.) I don't want to go to the playroom!

Therapist: It is time to go to the playroom.

The therapist starts by giving a command rather than responding to Jason's behavior and feelings.

Therapist: It is your time in the playroom and we are going now.	The therapist does not respond to Jason's feelings and seems to allow their own frustration come out in the response.
Jason: (With arms still folded and head still down.) I don't have to go if I don't want to.	Jason becomes more adamant in his decision to avoid the playroom.
Therapist: (Begins to take his hand and says) It is time to go, follow me, I will show you where the playroom is. (Jason and therapist enter the playroom and Jason begins exploring the toys in the room.)	Again the therapist does not respond to Jason's feelings and takes control of the session and the child's actions.
Jason: I don't see anything I want to play with.	Jason is still expressing his feelings of anger and aggression.
Therapist: You don't see anything you like.	The therapist responds with a reflection of content but does not acknowledge Jason's feelings.
Jason: (Sees the gun and seems to get excited.) I know what I can do. I can shoot this gun!	Jason finally begins to play with the toys.
Therapist: You can shoot the gun but not at me.	The therapist sets a limit before it is needed. This may send the message to Jason that the therapist does not trust Jason's ability to make choices for himself regarding aggression toward others.
Jason: (Points the gun at the therapist.) I can, too, if I want to!	The therapist's response again triggers Jason's anger and his desire to control the session by doing the opposite of what the therapist says.
Therapist: If you choose to shoot the gun at me, you choose not to play with the gun for the rest of our playtime.	The therapist sets the ultimate limit too soon, again sending the message that the therapist does not trust Jason. The therapist also fails to acknowledge Jason's feelings.

Jason: (With anger in his voice.) I can too! (Then he shoots the dart toward the therapist.)	Jason's anger increases.
Therapist: I told you the gun was not for shooting at me, since you chose to shoot at me, you chose not to play with the gun anymore today.	The therapist fails to acknowledge Jason's feelings and takes control of the session by controlling Jason's behavior. By taking the gun away, the therapist confirms that they do not trust Jason to follow limits and express his anger/aggression in a way that does not hurt the therapist or himself.
Jason: (yelling) But I want to still play with it.	Jason's anger continues to increase.
Therapist: (Therapist heads toward Jason to put the gun on a high shelf.) It is time to put the gun on the shelf for the rest of today.	The therapist still failed to acknowledge the child's feelings.
Jason: (Draws a fist and aims toward therapist.) I don't want to put it up!	The child is acting out his anger and aggression.
Therapist: (Removes gun from his hand and puts it on a shelf.) The gun is not for using for the rest of the day.	The therapist is in control of the session.
Jason: (In a very loud voice.) I don't like you and I don't like this place! I want to go home.	The child is expressing his anger and frustration at the events that have taken place in the playroom.
Therapist: It is not time to leave the playroom yet.	The therapist still has not reflected Jason's feelings. This may send the message that Jason's feelings are not important to the therapist. Also, the therapist's responses may send the message that it is more important for Jason to do what the therapist wants him to rather than for Jason to be free to express his feelings and thoughts in a safe environment.

CORRECTED INTERACTION

Excerpt #2: Therapist reflects the child's feelings and uses the ACT model.

Jason: (With arms folded and head down.) I don't want to go to the playroom!

Therapist: (Bends down to child's level.) You're not sure about going to the playroom but it is time to go to the playroom.

The therapist starts by getting on Jason's eye level in order to connect with him. The therapist then responds to Jason's feelings, which lets him know his feelings are important but also lets Jason know that it is time to go to the playroom.

Jason: NO! I am not going!

Jason continues to express his feelings.

Therapist: You really don't want to go but it is time to go to the playroom. You can choose to walk to the playroom by yourself or you can choose to walk to the playroom holding my hand.

The therapist now uses the ACT limit-setting model to acknowledge Jason's feelings and give choices to him. This allows Jason to express his feelings and begin to make choices in how he is going to deal with his feelings and the choices presented by the therapist.

Jason: I can walk all by myself! (Runs toward the playroom.)

Although Jason is still expressing some anger, he is making choices within the limits and this helps prevent a power struggle between the therapist and child.

Therapist: (Following Jason to the playroom.) You decided to walk to the playroom all on your own. (Jason and therapist have now entered the playroom and Jason begins exploring the toys in the room.)

This response continues to let Jason know that the therapist is focused on him.

Jason: I don't see anything I want to play with.

Therapist: You're disappointed because you don't see what you want to play with.

Reflections of Jason's affect are important in the child-centered approach. In this response the therapist responds to Jason's feelings, which facilitates an environment where Jason can feel safe to express himself.

Jason: (Sees the gun and seems to get excited.) I know what I can do. I can shoot this gun!

Jason is beginning to make decisions for himself in the playroom.

Therapist: You found something you like and know how to use it.

The therapist continues to acknowledge Jason's feelings. The therapist also gives Jason credit for knowing how to use the gun without jumping to the conclusion that he will use the gun inappropriately.

Jason: (Points the gun at the therapist.) I can shoot you.

Jason begins to test the limits in the playroom.

Therapist: Jason, I know you would like to shoot the gun at me, but I am not for shooting. You can choose to shoot the door or the wall.

The therapist calmly sets a limit using the ACT model.

Jason: (With anger in his voice.) I can too!

Jason continues to challenge the limit and express his anger.

Therapist: I know you are angry, but I am not for shooting. You can choose to shoot the door or the wall.

The therapist uses the ACT limit-setting model. The therapist sets the limit in a calm voice sending the message that the therapist trusts Jason's ability to make choices for himself. It also lets Jason know that his anger is acceptable and does not make him wrong.

Jason: (Points the gun at the sandbox and pulls the trigger.) I'll shoot it in here.

Although Jason still seems to be challenging the therapist, Jason is able to make a decision that helps him feel in control and follows the limits of the playroom. Additionally, Jason's anger has decreased.

Therapist: You found a place to shoot the gun and you got it right in there.

The therapist recognizes Jason's ability to find an appropriate place to shoot the gun.

Jason: (Looking for the dart he shot in the sandbox.) I sure did! And I can do it again.

Jason's anger has dissipated and is replaced with excitement. He seems to be connecting with the therapist and begins to become more comfortable in the playroom.

Therapist: You like the shot you made and decided to shoot some more.

This response continues to reflect Jason's feelings and encourage his decision-making ability.

Jason: (Leaves the gun and begins to explore other toys in the room.) Maybe there is something else I can play with.

Jason now feels safe enough to explore the playroom even more.

Therapist: You decided you want to play with some of the other toys in the room.

This reflection of content continues to let Jason know that the therapist is fully present and focused on him.

EXCERPT FROM PLAY THERAPY SESSION TWO

Learning Objective — for the play therapist to avoid parroting

This excerpt shows the significance of therapeutic responses that do not mimic the child. In the first excerpt, the therapist simply parrots Jason's actions and verbalizations and fails to respond to the deeper messages Jason may be sending. In the second section, the therapist responds to Jason on a deeper level.

INITIAL INTERACTION

Excerpt #1: Therapist parroted the child's actions and verbalizations.

Introduction to the Session

This excerpt occurs fifteen minutes into the session. Jason entered the playroom willingly but still continued to express anger. Jason's play seems to become more focused during the following section.

Jason: (Building a scene in the sandbox using animals.) This is the good guy and this is the bad guy.

Therapist: That is the good guy and that is the bad guy.

This response is a reflection of content. However, the response is a verbatim account of what the child said. This may make the session seem as if the therapist is more focused on the use of "proper techniques" rather than what the child is expressing.

Jason: (Continues to build his scene with his back toward the therapist; sets up several other toys in the sandbox facing each other.)

Therapist: You are setting those up the way you want them.

The therapist acknowledges Jason's actions.

Jason: (The bad guy goes toward the good guy in a loud, angry voice.) You are mean! You have to do what I say or else!

Jason begins to act out some of his feelings through his play in the sandbox.

Therapist: He says that one is mean and he better do what he says.

The therapist responds to Jason's verbalization using a reflection of content. However, the response seems somewhat mechanical and overlooks the feelings that Jason is expressing.

Jason: (The bad guy is now jumping on the good guy.) I'm going to get you! You better do what I say!

Jason is involved in his play. Jason's lack of verbal response does not indicate that Jason does not feel connected to the therapist. Many times the child may not respond to what the therapist says during a session.

Therapist: You are making him jump on that one and he is getting him.

The therapist continues to respond to Jason's actions (tracking). Although this response is on target, the therapist can take the session deeper by responding to any feelings that Jason may be expressing.

Jason: (Looks toward therapist.) He gets really mad when he doesn't do what he is supposed to.

This is Jason's way of connecting with the therapist.

Therapist: He gets mad when he doesn't do what he is supposed to.

The therapist's response is mechanical and does not reflect a deeper understanding of what Jason is expressing.

Jason: (With a sad look in his eyes and in a soft voice.) Yeah when he gets mad he hits things. (Looks back at the toys and has them start fighting.)

Therapist: So when he gets mad he hits. Now they are fighting.

The therapist's response is mechanical and does not reflect a deeper understanding of what Jason is expressing.

Jason: (As the good guy and bad guy are fighting, the bad guy says:) Take that! (The good guy says:) No, you take that!

Therapist: They are getting each other.

Acknowledges Jason's actions (tracking response).

Jason: (Throws the good guy down and holds up the bad guy and with excitement says:) I won!

Therapist: The bad guy beat the good guy.

Reflection of content. This response does not acknowledge Jason's feelings.

CORRECTED INTERACTION

Excerpt #2: Therapist uses a variety of therapeutic responses to deepen the session.

Jason: (Building a scene in the sandbox using animals.) This is the good guy and this is the bad guy.

Therapist: You decided one is good and one is bad.

This response focuses on Jason's decision-making ability. This is a deeper response than a reflection of content that parrots Jason's verbalization.

Jason: (Continues to build his scene; sets up several other toys in the sandbox facing each other.)

Therapist: You are setting those up the way you want them.

Acknowledges Jason's actions (tracking response).

Jason: (The bad guy goes toward the good guy in a loud, angry voice.) You are mean! You have to do what I say or else!

Jason begins to play out some feelings during the session.

Therapist: Sounds like that one is mad and wants to get his way.

This response focuses on the underlying feelings that Jason is expressing. By focusing on feelings, the therapist is able to help Jason identify and express his feelings.

Jason: (The bad guy is now jumping on the good guy.) I'm going to get you! You better do what I say!

Therapist: The bad guy really wants to make sure the good guy does what he says.

This response again focuses on the meaning of Jason's play. This helps Jason begin to work through the feelings he is expressing.

Jason: (Looks toward therapist.) He gets really mad when he doesn't do what he is supposed to.

Therapist: You know just what happens when he gets mad.

This response focuses on Jason's interpretation of the play and what is happening.

Jason: (With a sad look in his eyes and in a soft voice.) Yeah when he gets mad he hits things. (Looks back at the toys and has them start fighting.)

Therapist: You feel sad when he gets mad and hits things.

This response focuses on Jason's feelings about the play rather than the action of the play. Focusing on the feeling helps take the session to a deeper level.

Jason: (As the good guy and bad guy are fighting, the bad guy says:) Take that! (The good guy says:) No, you take that!

Therapist: Seems like they are really mad at each other.   Reflection of feeling.

Jason: (Throws the good guy down and holds up the bad guy and with excitement says:) I won!

Therapist: You're really excited that he won.   Reflection of feeling.

CHAPTER 17

CASE STUDY: DIVORCE

Sally, a six-year-old girl, was brought to counseling by her mother and father and stepmother. Sally's parents divorced when she was two years old. Her father had remarried and his second wife was pregnant. All three parents wanted to be involved in the play therapy process. Sally's mother became engaged to her fiancé while Sally was in play therapy. Sally's stepmother reported that she wanted to make sure that Sally adjusted well to the new sibling and the new marriage. Sally's father reported that he was concerned about how Sally responded to the divorce and how she responded to each parent.

In the therapeutic setting, Sally was very quiet and focused on arts and crafts activities. Sally's play was also extremely neat and controlled. She seldom spoke to the therapist during the session but was very vocal to and from the playroom. Sally seemed to display behaviors that were far above her developmental age. Throughout the play therapy process Sally became more active and messy in the playroom.

EXCERPT FROM PLAY THERAPY SESSION ONE

Learning Objective — for the play therapist to respond to the child despite the absence of verbalization from the child

In the first excerpt, the therapist tries to force Sally to be more vocal during the session. Many beginning play therapists have difficulty working with a child that is not very verbal during the play session. The child should feel free to use the time in the playroom the way the child wants to. In the corrected section, the therapist responds to Sally's actions in the playroom without forcing her to interact the way the therapist wants.

INITIAL INTERACTION

Excerpt #1: In the following excerpt, the therapist does not follow the child's lead and tries to elicit verbal responses from the child.

Sally: (Enters the playroom and looks around. Goes to the table with the arts and crafts materials.)

Therapist: You found the paper and crayons. Do you like to draw?

The first part of this response is a tracking response. The second part is an unnecessary question. The question is not needed to further the session.

Sally: Yeah. (Begins to draw a picture without looking at the therapist. Covers the picture with her hand as she draws.)

Therapist: Looks like you are drawing something very important to you. I wonder what it is.

The first part of the response is acknowledging actions (tracking behavior); however, the therapist may be assuming that the picture may be more significant than Sally intended. The second part of the response implies that Sally needs to share with the therapist what her picture is. This takes the lead away from Sally.

Sally: (Without responding to the therapist, moves to the easel to paint.)

Therapist: You decided to paint now. You really like to make things.

Facilitation of decision-making.

Sally: (Begins to carefully paint a rainbow using all the colors. Makes sure the colors do not mix, puts a flower underneath the rainbow, and a sun in the corner.)

Therapist: You are making a rainbow with lots of colors. Do you paint rainbows at school and home?

First part of the response focuses on Sally's actions and behaviors. The therapist tries to engage Sally in conversation by asking another question. This may send the message that it is not okay for Sally to be silent during the session.

Sally: Sometimes. (Finishes her painting and goes back to the arts and crafts table and starts to finish her first picture she started.)

Therapist: So you like to paint rainbows at school and home. Looks like you are ready to finish your other picture.

Sally: Yeah. I want to take it home with me.

Therapist: You want to take it home and maybe share it with your mom and dad.

First part of this response is a reflection of content. In the second part, the therapist assumes what Sally's intentions are for the picture. This may communicate that there is an appropriate or correct action for Sally to take with the picture.

Sally: (As she is coloring she puts back each crayon and does not leave anything out on the table.)

Therapist: You are putting everything back. You must keep things very clean at home and school.

The therapist generalizes Sally's behavior to situations outside the playroom. This again may be an attempt by the therapist to encourage Sally to be more vocal. During the session, it is important to keep the focus on Sally and her actions during the session, not what occurs outside of the session.

Sally: Sometimes. (Turns from the table and begins to look around the room at other toys in the room.)

Therapist: Looks like you might like to do something else. You can play with the toys if you want to.

The therapist seems to be encouraging certain behaviors. The therapist should allow Sally the time needed to decide how Sally would like to spend her time during the session.

CORRECTED INTERACTION

Excerpt #2: Therapist follows the child's lead and does not force verbalization by the child.

This interaction shows how the therapist can follow the child's lead and still be interacting with the child even when the child does not verbalize anything during the session.

Sally: (Enters the playroom and looks around. Goes to the table with the arts and crafts materials)

Therapist: Looks like you found something you want to do.

This response focuses on where Sally is in the session without implying she needs to use the materials in any certain way.

Sally: (Begins to draw a picture without looking at the therapist. Covers the picture with her hand as she draws.)

Therapist: You are working hard on your picture.

This response focuses on Sally's work and effort and not the product.

Sally: (Without responding to the therapist, moves to the easel to paint.)

Therapist: You're ready to do something different and you found what you want.

This response focuses on Sally's ability to make choices and use the session the way she wants. This also lets Sally know that the therapist does not have any expectations for Sally's behavior.

Sally: (Begins to carefully paint a rainbow using all the colors. Makes sure the colors do not mix, puts a flower underneath the rainbow, and a sun in the corner.)

Therapist: You are working carefully on that. You want to make sure it is just the way you want it.

The therapist responds to the effort and work Sally is putting into her pictures. Although Sally is not verbally communicating, the therapist is working hard to communicate with Sally.

167

Sally: (Finishes her painting and steps back and looks at her painting. Goes back to the arts and crafts table and starts to finish the first picture she started.)

Therapist: You are checking out your painting. Looks like you are pleased with your picture.

This response focuses on Sally's feelings about her picture. This shows how Sally can express her feeling without using words. Play therapists must focus on all actions that happen during the session in order to fully understand the child.

Sally: Can I take this home with me?

Therapist: That is something you can decide.

This response allows Sally to decide what she would like to do with her picture.

Sally: (As she is coloring she puts back each crayon and does not leave anything out on the table.)

Therapist: You want to make sure you put things back when you are finished with them.

This response focuses on Sally's actions during the session. It lets Sally know that the therapist is fully focused on her throughout the session.

Sally: (Turns from the table and begins to look around the room at other toys in the room.)

Therapist: You are looking to see what else is in this room.

This response focuses on her actions but does not force her to use the materials in any certain way. This allows Sally to stay in the lead of the session.

EXCERPT FROM PLAY THERAPY SESSION FOUR

Learning Objective — for the play therapist to follow the child's lead

This excerpt shows the significance of following the child's lead even when the child is not verbal. In the first excerpt, the therapist takes the lead of the session by trying to engage Sally in other activities in hopes to have more direct interaction with her. In the second section, the therapist follows Sally's lead.

INITIAL INTERACTION

Excerpt #1: Therapist takes the lead from the child and directs the activities of the session.

Introduction to the Session

This excerpt occurs during the fourth session. Sally continues to use the arts and crafts materials but has begun to use other materials. Sally also began to leave toys out after she used them.

Sally: (Playing in the sandbox; sifts sand through a slotted spoon into a bucket.)

Therapist: You are putting that right in there. You can use the other toys in the sandbox.

The therapist is beginning to direct the session by encouraging the use of other materials. The child centered play therapist trusts that the child will use what they need to during the session to express themselves.

Sally: (Continues to sift sand; as she is playing some sand falls onto the floor of the playroom; she stops her play to look at the therapist.)

Sally may not be sure if it is ok for things to get messy in the playroom. Her previous behavior in the playroom shows that she has a tendency to be very neat in her play.

Therapist: You noticed some sand fell on the floor. There is a broom over there (points to the broom and dustpan) if you don't like the sand on the floor or you can just leave it there.

The therapist assumes that Sally wants to clean the floor based on previous sessions. This again takes the lead away from the child and does not allow Sally to deal with the mess in the way that she may want.

169

Sally: Okay. (Goes to get the broom and begins sweeping up the sand that fell on the floor.)

Therapist: You decided to sweep it up. Tell me how you help clean at home.

The therapist is trying to get Sally to become more vocal. In the playroom it is the child's choice to speak or not to speak. The therapist needs to become comfortable with a non-verbal child. A non-verbal child still communicates with the therapist through their activity.

Sally: Sometimes I help Mom clean up the kitchen. I just play at Dad's house.

Therapist: So you help clean at your mom's but not very much at your dad's.

The therapist is using reflection of content but the information Sally is sharing is based on the therapist taking the lead from the child.

Sally: Yeah. I do have to clean my room at my dad's house. Mom doesn't like for the house to be messy so I keep all my toys in my room.

Therapist: You have different rules at each house. Do you like to keep things clean or do you like to leave your toys out?

The therapist continues to take the lead of the session by asking questions. Sally will communicate what she needs to during the session through her play. It is not necessary to ask questions to satisfy the therapist's need for information.

Sally: I don't know. (Begins to play in the sand again with her back toward the therapist; sifts the sand back into the bucket and feels the sand run through her hands.)

Sally is not interested in the direction the therapist is taking the session.

Therapist: You're not quite sure. Looks like you are ready to play in the sand some more.

Reflection of content and acknowledges actions (tracking behavior).

Sally: (Quietly plays in the sand; filling up the bucket then dumping the sand back out.)

Therapist: You seem to like the sand but there are lots of toys you can play with. We can even play something together if you like.

The therapist tries to direct the session by suggesting other activities in the playroom. The therapist is meeting her own needs of how she thinks the session should unfold by engaging the child in more interactive activities.

Sally: Okay. (Turns toward therapist ~~but still has hands~~ in the sand.)

Sally may feel that she has to participate in the activities.

Therapist: There is a dollhouse right there, we could play dolls.

The therapist is now in complete lead of the session. Sally is no longer able to address the issues she wants to during the play therapy session.

CORRECTED INTERACTION

Excerpt #2: Therapist follows the child's lead and does not force verbalization by the child.

This interaction shows how the therapist can follow the child's lead and still be interacting with the child even when the child does not verbalize during the session. This interaction also shows how Sally's play has changed over the four play sessions.

Sally: (Playing in the sandbox; sifts sand through a slotted spoon into a bucket.)

Therapist: You are putting that right in there.

Acknowledges actions (tracking response). Lets Sally know that the therapist is focused on her.

Sally: (Continues to sift sand; as she is playing some sand falls onto the floor of the playroom; she stops her play to look at the therapist.)

Sally may not be sure if it is okay for things to get messy in the playroom. Her previous behavior in the playroom shows that she has a tendency to be very neat in her play.

Therapist: You're not quite sure about that sand falling on the floor. Sometimes sand gets on the floor.	The therapist responds to Sally's feelings in this response. The therapist also lets Sally know that she can decide how to handle the sand on the floor and that it is okay for things to get dirty in the playroom.
Therapist: You really like playing in the sand.	By responding to Sally's feelings about her sand play, the therapist sends the message that she is present and that Sally's decision to leave the sand on the floor is okay in the playroom.
Sally: (Looks around the room and puts more toys in the sandbox; begins to pour sand from the bucket into pots and pans from the kitchen area.)	Sally feels free to use the materials in the playroom. She is beginning to explore the playroom and use more materials in the playroom.
Therapist: Putting those in there and pouring the sand into them.	Acknowledges actions (tracking response).
Sally: (Takes the pot and pan of sand to the stove and begins to cook; seems pleased with her idea.)	
Therapist: You're cooking something right on there and you are having fun.	The therapist continues to follow Sally's lead and respond to any feelings Sally expresses, even non-verbally. Children express many things through their activities in the playroom. The therapist must learn to listen with his or her eyes, not just the ears.
Sally: (Continues to cook, then puts food on two plates and cups; brings one to the therapist and keeps one for herself.)	Sally is now making a connection with the therapist. This shows how the child can connect without words.
Therapist: You made both of us something to eat.	This response focuses on how the child is connecting to the therapist.
Sally: (Pretends to eat her food; then starts to clean up the food toys and dump the sand back in the sandbox, as she does some more sand falls on the floor.)	

Therapist: All finished. Now you decided to put it back in there.

The therapist is focused on Sally's behavior. Sally continues to become more comfortable and does not even react to the sand falling on the floor. The therapist has created an environment where Sally can get messy when Sally is ready. This shows progress she is making in therapy.

CHAPTER 18

CASE STUDY: SEXUAL ABUSE AND TRAUMA

Five-year-old Becky was brought to play therapy by her mother due to sexual abuse and trauma. Becky was sexually abused by Joey, an eight-year-old boy. Prior to the sexual abuse, Becky and her mother had been close friends with Joey and his mother. Becky's mother reported the abuse to child protective services and was seeking play therapy to help Becky. Becky's mother also stated that Becky often told people that she was abused even if she did not know them very well. In addition to the sexual abuse, Becky experienced a traumatic event when she was four years old. Becky's mother passed out and Becky called 9-1-1 to get help.

In the therapeutic setting, Becky was very vocal and active during the session. Becky talked about her abuse during the first play therapy session, but did not discuss it after that point. She interacted frequently with the therapist and often played out her experiences from the week.

EXCERPT FROM PLAY THERAPY SESSION ONE

Learning Objective — for the play therapist to reflect the child's feelings and integrate the use of different types of therapeutic responses

In the first excerpt, the therapist misses opportunities to reflect the child's feelings and other therapeutic responses. In the corrected section, the therapist uses appropriate therapeutic responses.

INITIAL INTERACTION

Excerpt #1: In the following excerpt, the therapist does not reflect the child's feelings.

This interaction occurs ten minutes into the first play therapy session. Becky has explored the toys in the room and found some that are interesting to her. She has been very vocal during the session.

Becky: (Picks up the medical kit.)
I know what this is for.

Therapist: You know what that is used for; looks like you are going to use it in here.

The therapist begins the session with reflections of content.

Becky: (As she is looking through the medical kit, she states:) Joey made sex with me.

Becky's mother reported that Becky often told people that she did not know well about her sexual abuse. Mom felt Becky was too open about her experiences.

Therapist: He did. Tell me what happened.

The therapist is searching for information at this point. When dealing with sexual abuse, therapists often feel they need to gather more information or "fix" the child's feelings about the abuse. In child-centered play therapy, the therapist follows the lead of the child and trusts they will express what they need to during session to deal with the abuse.

Becky: He made sex with me at his house then I told Mommy and he got in trouble.

Becky tells the therapist her understanding about what happened. This shows how searching for information may not always produce the results the therapist wants.

Therapist: So you know it was not okay for Joey to do that to you.

The therapist is in an education mode. The therapist is teaching Becky about good touch versus secret touch. Although this is important information for Becky to have, the playroom is a place where Becky should be allowed to express her feelings the way she needs to.

Becky: (Walks toward therapist with the shot from medical kit.) Yeah. Mommy told me that is why I get to come here to play.

Therapist: So you know you are coming here to talk about what Joey did to you.

The therapist reflects the content but begins to lead the child by reinforcing what Becky's mother has told her. In the playroom, Becky should be allowed to deal with her feelings the way she wants to, not be forced to talk about the abuse.

Becky: Yeah. (Hands the shot to the therapist, pulls up her dress to show her hip to the therapist.) You be the doctor and give me a shot right here.

Becky begins to play. Becky is beginning to show how her boundaries may be slightly lower than other children her age.

Therapist: Okay. (Takes the shot and gives Becky a shot in the hip.) Now let's put a Band-Aid on your shot.

The therapist engages in the play and neglects to redirect Becky's desire to have the shot given in her hip (underneath her dress). The therapist needs to redirect Becky to be given the shot in another location (arm/hand). Instead, the therapist allows Becky the opportunity to continue her play while not maintaining appropriate boundaries.

Becky: Now it is my turn to give you a shot. (Begins to pull on the therapist's clothes to give a shot on the hip.)

Therapist: I don't want a shot on my hip. You can pick another place to give me a shot.

The therapist should set their own personal boundaries during the session. When setting their own boundaries, the therapist needs to acknowledge that it is their own limit and does not have to do with their acceptance of the child. The therapist should also offer acceptable alternatives for the child to choose from.

Becky: But you always get a shot in the hip at the doctor's office. So I want to give you one on the hip too.

Therapist: I don't want a shot. You can listen to my heart instead. (Looks through the medical kit and hands Becky the stethoscope.)

The therapist misses an opportunity to respond to Becky's feelings. By redirecting Becky's behavior, the therapist is leading the session and rescuing Becky from dealing with her disappointment.

Becky: Okay. (Puts on the stethoscope to listen to the therapist's heart.) I hear your heart it is beating fast.

Therapist: You can hear mine. Now I can listen to yours too if you want.

The therapist is continuing to participate in the play even though Becky has not asked for the therapist to continue.

CORRECTED INTERACTION

Excerpt #2: Therapist reflects the child's feelings.

Becky: (Picks up the medical kit.) I know what this is for.

Therapist: You know what that is used for; looks like you are going to use it in here.

The therapist begins the session with reflections of content.

Becky: (As she is looking through the medical kit, she states:) Joey made sex with me.

Becky's mother reported that she often told other people, even those she did not know very well about her sexual abuse. Mom felt Becky was too open about her experiences.

Therapist: You know what Joey did to you but you didn't like it.

The therapist focuses on Becky's feelings at this point. This allows her to go where she wants in order to express her feelings about the abuse.

Becky: No. He can't do it anymore. I don't play with Joey anymore. (In a sad tone of voice. Walking toward therapist with the medical kit.)

Becky feels free to tell the therapist what she wants to and how the abuse has impacted her.

Therapist: So you know that Joey can't hurt you anymore. Seems like you are a little sad you don't get to play with Joey anymore.

The therapist reflects the feelings Becky may be expressing. At times, it may be difficult to identify feelings in the play therapy session. However, as a therapist tries to identify a child's feelings, the child will let the therapist know if they are on target.

Becky: (Opens the medical kit in front of the therapist; hands the shot to the therapist, pulls up her dress to show her hip to the therapist.) You be the doctor and give me a shot right here.

Becky has moved on to different play.

Therapist: I know you want me to give you a shot there, but I choose not to give you a shot on the hip. You can choose for me to give you a shot on your hand or on your arm.

The therapist uses the ACT limit-setting model to set their own personal limit within the session. It is important that the therapist model how to set boundaries when necessary. This also allows the therapist to remain accepting of the child.

Becky: (Lowers her dress and roles up her sleeve.) Okay give me a shot in my arm.

Becky responds to the therapist.

Therapist: Show me how you want me to give you the shot.

The therapist engages in the play as Becky asks. By asking Becky how she wants the therapist to give the shot, the therapist keeps Becky in the lead of the session.

Becky: (Gives the shot to the therapist then uses her finger to show the therapist how to give the shot.) You put it up here and push.

Therapist: (Gives Becky the shot.) So you put it up here and push like this.

The therapist follows Becky's lead and joins in the play only as asked and does not take the play further than Becky directed.

Becky: (Takes the shot and puts it up to the therapist's arm.) Now I am going to give you a shot.

Therapist: You decided to give me one just like you.

The therapist focuses on the connection Becky is making by giving a shot just like she received.

Becky: Yeah. (Puts on the stethoscope to listen to the therapist's heart.) I can hear your heart with this.

Therapist: You know how to use that. You are proud that you know how to use all of those.

The therapist responds to Becky's feelings.

In the corrected section, the therapist does not push Becky to discuss her sexual abuse. Instead, she allows her to deal with her feelings and thoughts as she is ready to address them. Although Becky did not talk about the abuse long, the therapist has created an environment that lets her know she can talk when she is ready. Becky did not discuss her abuse after this point in the therapy process. Instead, she focused on her feelings associated with her experiences in her day-to-day life.

EXCERPT FROM PLAY THERAPY SESSION SIX

Learning Objective — for the play therapist to participate in the play only as directed by the child

In the first excerpt, the therapist participates in the child's play and pushes the child for the meaning of the play. This is the first time Becky has played this scene in the playroom. In the corrected section, the therapist participates in the play as the child asks and does not try to force the child to explain the meaning of her play.

INITIAL INTERACTION

Excerpt #1: In the following excerpt, the therapist engages in the play with the child and tries to get the child to explain the meaning of her play.

Becky: I want to play cops. (Goes to the shelf and picks up the handcuffs.)

Therapist: You know just what you want to do today.

Facilitation of decision-making.

Becky: (Picks up the gun and puts it in her pocket; puts on the police hat and walks toward therapist.) Now you are the bad guy and you are going to jail.

Therapist: Bad people go to jail. What things do bad people do that make them have to go to jail?

The therapist is trying to get Becky to explain her play. In the playroom, the child's play should speak for itself.

The therapist may not always understand what the play means. If the therapist creates a safe environment, the child will play out what the child needs to even if the therapist does not understand the meaning.

Becky: (In a deep voice.) Put out your hands. You are going to jail.

Therapist: You are taking me to jail. What did I do that I have to go to jail? (Puts out her hands and Becky puts the handcuffs on her hands.)

Again the therapist is searching for the meaning of the play and trying to get Becky to explain her actions. The therapist should trust the child and focus on what Becky is expressing rather than why she is playing cops.

Becky: You know what you did! Now let's go. (Pulls at therapist's arm to get her to stand up.)

Therapist: (Stands up and follows Becky.) You are taking me to jail now. You know what happens to bad people.

Reflection of content. The therapist is following the child's lead but has allowed herself to be put in a position where she may not be able to view all of Becky's actions in the playroom.

Becky: (Walks therapist around the room and then puts her behind the puppet theater.) Now stay there until I tell you to come out.

Therapist: You put me right here in jail. How long do bad people stay in jail?

Continues to press Becky for the reasons behind her play.

Becky: (Riding on the car.) I'm going out to look for more bad people. (Pulls up to the puppet theater and takes therapist back out.) Now it is your turn to be the cop and my turn to be the bad guy.

Therapist: Now we are going to switch. What am I putting you in jail for?

The therapist continues to question Becky even though Becky has not responded to any of the therapist's previous questions. When the therapist asks questions, the therapist is directing the therapeutic process and the child is not free to choose specific concerns to address through play.

Becky: (Takes off handcuffs and hands them to therapist.) Because I am the bad guy. Now you put these on me.

Therapist: What did you do to make you the bad guy? (Begins to put the handcuffs on Becky.)

The therapist continues to question Becky. In order to encourage Becky to direct the therapeutic process, the therapist needed to ask Becky how Becky wanted the handcuffs put on (i.e., Behind her back or in front of her body.) Even when asked to participate in play, the therapist should allow the child to lead how the play will be carried out.

Becky: (With handcuffs on, walks toward the puppet theater.) Now it is time for me to go to jail.

Therapist: Now you are in jail and you better stay there.

Begins to role-play in the child's play but does not follow Becky's lead.

CORRECTED INTERACTION

Excerpt #2: Therapist follows the child's lead without trying to get the child to explain the meaning behind the play.

Becky: I want to play cops. (Goes to the shelf and picks up the handcuffs.)

Therapist: You know just what you want to do today.

Facilitation of decision-making.

Becky: (Picks up the gun and puts it in her pocket; puts on the police hat and walks toward therapist.) Now you are the bad guy and you are going to jail.

Therapist: You've decided I am the bad guy and you are taking me to jail.

The therapist simply follows Becky's lead without trying to get her to explain the reasons behind her play. The child-centered therapist trusts the child to express him or herself.

Becky: (In a deep voice.) Put out your hands. You are going to jail.

Therapist: (Puts out her hands and Becky puts the handcuffs on her hands.) You know just how to make those work and you are putting them right on me.

The therapist continues to follow Becky's lead and also uses an encouraging response about her ability to use the toys in the playroom.

Becky: (Pulls at therapist's arm to get her to stand up.) Now let's go. It is time to take you to jail.

Therapist: (Stays in her chair.) I know you would like to take me to jail but I choose to stay in my chair. You can choose to pretend the chair is jail.

ACT limit-setting model. The therapist sets a limit on moving around the room. This allows the therapist to remain in a position where she can fully see the activity of Becky during the play session.

Becky: (Pretends to take therapist to jail.) Now stay there until I tell you to come out.

Therapist: You are in charge and put me right here in jail.

The therapist responds to Becky's desire to be in control.

Becky: (Riding on the car.) I'm going out to look for more bad people. (Pulls up to the therapist and takes the handcuffs off.) Now it is your turn to be the cop and my turn to be the bad guy.

Therapist: Now we are going to switch; you are making me the cop and you are the one in trouble.

The therapist follows Becky's lead.

Becky: (Begins to put handcuffs on herself.) Now I am the bad guy and I have to go to jail. (Walks over to the puppet theater and sits down with a sad look on her face.)

Therapist: You decided to be in jail right behind there. You don't like being in jail.

The therapist follows Becky's lead and responds to her feelings. Although the therapist may not understand why Becky has started this type of play, she trusts that she is expressing herself the way she needs.

Becky: (Comes out from behind puppet theater and takes off handcuffs.) Let's do something else. (Walks toward paints.)

Therapist: All finished with that and now you are ready to do something else.

Reflection of content.

In this section the therapist used several therapeutic responses to allow Becky to express what she needed to. This was the first time Becky had played out this scene. Although the therapist did not understand the play the therapist did not push for an explanation. After the session the therapist held a parent consultation. Becky's mother reported that Becky's father was arrested in front of their house during the past week due to driving under the influence. This illustrates how Becky was using the playroom to work through her daily life experiences. The therapist did not need to know why Becky was playing cops in order to create an environment where she could express her feelings about the situation. By using therapeutic responses, Becky expressed herself the way she needed.

TRAINING AND SUPERVISION

This section is designed for the supervisor of play therapists in training and clinical practice.

The first part of the training and supervision section provides a basic foundation for learning and integrating the fundamental skills of child-centered play therapy. The six skills listed below are introduced and practiced one at a time.

- Acknowledging Non-Verbal Actions
- Reflecting Content
- Reflecting Feeling
- Facilitating Esteem-Building and Encouragement
- Facilitating Decision-Making and Self-Responsibility
- Limit-Setting

The second section provides video review and feedback forms to be utilized in supervision, self-supervision, or peer supervision. The initial forms focus on each of the six specific skills and two additional forms focus on the integration of the six therapeutic responses.

These forms are designed to be used while reviewing video tapes of play therapy sessions prior to a formal supervisory session. This type of review helps the play therapist gain a heightened awareness of the play therapist's strengths and areas for growth.

CHAPTER 19

ROLE-PLAY OF SKILLS AND FEEDBACK FORMAT

ROLE-PLAY: ACKOWLEDGING NON-VERBAL ACTIONS

Supervisor Models the Skill

1. First, the supervisor or instructor models the skill to the individual, group, or class.

2. Have an individual pretend to be a child and play with various *toys without talking.*

3. The supervisor or instructor uses conversational and genuine therapeutic responses to acknowledge the child's non-verbal actions several times.

   This skill is used when the child is not verbally communicating and other therapeutic responses such as facilitating esteem-building or decision-making cannot be used. Responses that acknowledge non-verbal actions let the child know that the therapist is present, cares, and wants to understand the child. It is a way of connecting and creating a safe and caring environment when the child is not verbally communicating.

   The play therapist describes what the play therapist sees the child doing in a genuine and conversational manner that sounds engaging.

   Child: The child is playing with the dollhouse and doll figures.

   Therapist: You're putting those two in there.

Individuals Practice in Dyads or Triads

4. Provide the individual, group, or class with an opportunity to practice this skill. If possible, divide into groups of three. One person role-plays a child, one person the play therapist, and one the observer. The observer writes each response the play therapist makes to the child.

Play Therapist Acknowledges Own Strengths and One Area for Growth

5. At the end of the two to three minute role-play, the play therapist states what he or she did effectively and what he or she would like to change.

Observer Reviews Each of the Play Therapist's Responses

6. The observer reads aloud each of the play therapist's therapeutic responses and gives the copy of the responses to the play therapist.

Person Who Role-Played Child Reacts

7. The person who role-played the child gives specific feedback to the play therapist indicating how the play therapist's responses impacted him or her.

Observer: Use the numbered lines to write therapeutic responses.

Play Therapist: Use the second line (under the numbered lines) to make changes to your therapeutic response (if needed).

1. _____

_____

2. _____

_____

3. _____

_____

4. _____

_____

5. _____

_____

ROLE-PLAY: REFLECTING CONTENT

Supervisor Models the Skill

1. First, the supervisor or instructor models the skill to the individual, group, or class.

2. Have a person pretend to be a child and play with various toys. It is important that this individual verbalize the play process. (i.e., These two guys are angry at each other and they are going to have a fight.)

3. The supervisor or instructor uses conversational and genuine therapeutic responses to reflect content.

   This skill is used when the child is verbally communicating and other therapeutic responses such as facilitating esteem-building or decision-making cannot be used. Responses that reflect content let the child know that the therapist is listening and understands what is being said. Reflecting content provides another way to connect with the child while creating a safe and caring environment.

   The play therapist describes what the play therapist hears the child saying in a genuine and conversational manner.

Child:	(The child is playing with the dollhouse and doll figures.) These people (two adult figures) don't have much money. But they have a lot of love in their hearts. They are going to get these children who don't have any parents and take care of them.
Therapist:	The loving couple is going to take care of the children.

Individuals Practice in Dyads or Triads

4. Provide the individual, group, or class with an opportunity to practice this skill.

   If possible, divide into groups of three. One person role-plays a child, one person the play therapist, and one the observer. The observer writes each response the play therapist makes to the child.

Play Therapist Acknowledges Own Strengths and One Area for Growth

5. At the end of the two to three minute role-play, the play therapist states what he or she did effectively and what he or she would like to change.

Observer Reviews Each of the Play Therapist's Responses

6. The observer reads aloud each of the play therapist's therapeutic responses and gives the copy of the responses to the play therapist.

Person Who Role-Played Child Reacts

7. The person who role-played the child gives specific feedback to the play therapist indicating how the play therapist's responses impacted him or her.

Observer: Use the numbered lines to write therapeutic responses.

Play Therapist: Use the second line (under the numbered lines) to make changes to your therapeutic response (if needed).

1. _____

   _____

2. _____

   _____

3. _____

   _____

4. _____

   _____

5. _____

   _____

ROLE-PLAY: REFLECTING FEELING

Supervisor Models the Skill

1. First, the supervisor or instructor models the skill to the individual, group, or class.

2. Have a person pretend to be a child and play with various toys. It is important that this individual verbalize a play process that contains feeling. (i.e., The child may act excited to be in the playroom or frustrated that the child can't put two blocks together; the child may be using toys to express feelings of sadness, happiness, or anger.) This provides the therapist with an opportunity to reflect the feelings of the child or reflect the feelings of the toys or figures.

3. The supervisor or instructor uses conversational and genuine therapeutic responses to reflect feeling. The therapist's tone of voice matches the child's affect.

This skill is used when the child is communicating feelings. By identifying and acknowledging feelings, the child learns to become more aware of personal feelings and will be more capable of communicating feelings to others. The play therapist listens carefully to tone of voice, verbal communication, and observes non-verbal actions and facial gestures in order to accurately reflect the child's feelings. The child feels a deeper sense of feeling understood when the therapist accurately reflects the child's feelings.

Child: (The child is playing with the dollhouse and doll figures.) These people (two adult figures) don't have much money. But they have a lot of love in their hearts. They are going to get these children who don't have any parents and take care of them. (Tone of voice sounds happy.)

Therapist: The children are so happy that the loving couple is going to take care of them.

Individuals Practice in Dyads or Triads

4. Provide the individual, group, or class with an opportunity to practice this skill.

If possible, divide into groups of three. One person role-plays a child, one person the play therapist, and one the observer. The observer writes each response the play therapist makes to the child.

Play Therapist Acknowledges Own Strengths and One Area for Growth

5. At the end of the two to three minute role-play, the play therapist states what he or she did effectively and what he or she would like to change.

Observer Reviews Each of the Play Therapist's Responses

6. The observer reads aloud each of the play therapist's therapeutic responses and gives the copy of the responses to the play therapist.

Person Who Role-Played Child Reacts

7. The person who role-played the child gives specific feedback to the play therapist indicating how the play therapist's responses impacted him or her.

Observer: Use the numbered lines to write therapeutic responses.

Play Therapist: Use the second line (under the numbered lines) to make changes to your therapeutic response (if needed).

1. _____

   _____

2. _____

   _____

3. _____

   _____

4. _____

   _____

5. _____

   _____

ROLE-PLAY: INTEGRATING ACKNOWLEDGING NON-VERBAL ACTIONS, REFLECTING CONTENT AND REFLECTING FEELING

Supervisor Models the Skill

1. First, the supervisor or instructor models the integration of all three skills to the individual, group, or class.

2. Have a person pretend to be a child and play with various toys. It is important that the play contain action, verbal content, and feelings. This provides the therapist with an opportunity to illustrate all three skills.

3. The supervisor or instructor uses conversational and genuine therapeutic responses to acknowledge non-verbal actions, reflect content, and reflect feeling.

   The therapist is focused on building a relationship with the child while creating a safe and caring environment in which the child feels free to express feelings, concerns, and life experiences through play.

   The play therapist listens for opportunities to reflect the child's feelings and to reflect content. When opportunities do not exist to reflect feeling or content, the play therapist acknowledges the child's non-verbal actions in a genuine and conversational manner.

Child:	(Walks the two adult dolls into the house.)
Therapist:	You're walking those two into the house.
Child:	(The child is playing with the dollhouse and doll figures.) These people (two adult figures) don't have much money. But they have a lot of love in their hearts.
Therapist:	Although the couple doesn't have much money they still have a lot of love in them.
Child:	They are going to get these children who don't have any parents and take care of them. (Tone of voice sounds happy.)
Therapist:	The children are so happy that the loving couple is going to take care of them.

Individuals Practice in Dyads or Triads

4. Provide the individual, group, or class with an opportunity to practice integrating these three skills.

   If possible, divide into groups of three. One person role-plays a child, one person the play therapist, and one the observer. The observer writes each response the play therapist makes to the child.

Play Therapist Acknowledges Own Strengths and One Area for Growth

5. At the end of the five-minute role play, the play therapist states what he or she did effectively and what he or she would like to change.

Observer Reviews Each of the Play Therapist's Responses

6. The observer reads aloud each of the play therapist's therapeutic responses and gives the copy of the responses to the play therapist.

Person Who Role-Played Child Reacts

7. The person who role-played the child gives specific feedback to the play therapist indicating how the play therapist's responses impacted him or her.

Observer: Use the numbered lines to write therapeutic responses.

Play Therapist: Use the second line (under the numbered lines) to make changes to your therapeutic response (if needed).

1. _____

   _____

2. _____

   _____

3. _____

_____

4. _____

_____

5. _____

_____

6. _____

_____

7. _____

_____

8. _____

_____

9. _____

_____

ROLE-PLAY: FACILITATING ESTEEM-BUILDING AND ENCOURAGEMENT

Supervisor Models the Skill

1. First, the supervisor or instructor models the skill to the individual, group, or class.

2. Have a person pretend to be a child and play with various toys. It is important that this individual work toward accomplishing specific tasks. (i.e., The child puts a lot of effort into stacking blocks or balancing a soldier so that it stands in the military truck.) This provides the therapist with an opportunity to facilitate esteem-building and encouragement.

3. The supervisor or instructor uses conversational and genuine therapeutic responses to facilitate esteem-building and encouragement.

This skill is used to encourage a child's efforts and acknowledge the amount of work the child has put into a process. (i.e., The therapist acknowledges the process and effort put into drawing a picture, building a tower, etc.). By acknowledging the child's efforts, the child learns to internalize and acknowledge effort put into the process rather than looking to others for external praise and approval.

Child: (The child is playing with the dollhouse and doll figures. The child is spending several minutes dressing the adult figures in pants and shirts. Although the child is struggling at times, she is persistent and has not given up on the task. The child has also not asked the play therapist for help.) These clothes are hard to get on.

Therapist: You're working hard to get both of those people dressed.

Individuals Practice in Dyads or Triads

4. Provide the individual, group, or class with an opportunity to practice integrating these three skills.

   If possible, divide into groups of three. One person role-plays a child, one person the play therapist, and one the observer. The observer writes each response the play therapist makes to the child.

Play Therapist Acknowledges Own Strengths and One Area for Growth

5. At the end of the two to three minute role play, the play therapist states what he or she did effectively and what he or she would like to change.

Observer Reviews Each of the Play Therapist's Responses

6. The observer reads aloud each of the play therapist's therapeutic responses and gives the copy of the responses to the play therapist.

Person Who Role-Played Child Reacts

7. The person who role-played the child gives specific feedback to the play therapist indicating how the play therapist's responses impacted him or her.

Observer: Use the numbered lines to write therapeutic responses.

Play Therapist: Use the second line (under the numbered lines) to make changes to your therapeutic response (if needed).

1. _____

_____

2. _____

_____

3. _____

_____

4. _____

_____

5. _____

_____

ROLE-PLAY: FACILITATING DECISION-MAKING AND RESPONSIBILITY

Supervisor Models the Skill

1. First, the supervisor or instructor models the skill to the individual, group, or class.

2. Have a person pretend to be a child and play with various toys. It is important that this individual verbalize a play process that contains indecisiveness and dependence. (i.e., I don't know what to do. What should I play with? What is this thing for?) This type of verbalization provides the therapist with an opportunity to make responses that facilitate decision-making and responsibility.

3. The supervisor or instructor uses conversational and genuine therapeutic responses to facilitate decision-making and responsibility.

   This skill is used when the child is expressing a need for continual guidance and assistance and seems to have difficulty making decisions without the help of an adult. By making responses that facilitate decision-making and responsibility, the child learns to make age-appropriate decisions without the assistance of an adult and develop greater responsibility for his or her own actions.

Child:	(The child is looking at the dollhouse and holding several of the doll figures.) Which dolls should I play with?
Therapist:	You can decide which dolls you'd like to play with.

Individuals Practice in Dyads or Triads

4. Provide the individual, group, or class with an opportunity to practice this skill. If possible, divide into groups of three. One person role-plays a child, one person the play therapist, and one the observer. The observer writes each response the play therapist makes to the child.

Play Therapist Acknowledges Own Strengths and One Area for Growth

5. At the end of the two to three minute role play, the play therapist states what her or she did effectively and what he or she would like to have changed.

Observer Reviews Each of the Play Therapist's Responses

6. The observer reads aloud each of the play therapist's therapeutic responses and gives the copy of the responses to the play therapist.

Person Who Role-Played Child Reacts

7. The person who role-played the child gives specific feedback to the play therapist indicating how the play therapist's responses impacted him or her.

Observer: Use the numbered lines to write therapeutic responses.

Play Therapist: Use the second line (under the numbered lines) to make changes to your therapeutic response (if needed).

1. _____

   _____

2. _____

   _____

3. _____

   _____

4. _____

   _____

5. _____

   _____

ROLE-PLAY: LIMIT-SETTING

Supervisor Models the Skill

1. First, the supervisor or instructor models the skill to the individual, group, or class.

2. Have a person pretend to be a child and play with various toys. It is important that this individual provide the therapist opportunities to set limits (i.e., The child may be writing with a crayon on the desk. The child may act as though she is going to throw a plastic spider toward the therapist's face.) This provides the therapist with an opportunity to practice using the ACT model to set limits.

3. The supervisor or instructor uses a calm and firm voice to set limits.

This skill is used when the child is going to hurt himself or the therapist. the toys, the room, or is about to engage in a behavior that is socially unacceptable. By setting limits using the ACT model (Landreth, 2002), the child's feelings or desires are acknowledged (A) and the limit is stated in a clear and firm manner that diminishes the opportunity for power struggles (C). Lastly, the therapist targets an alternative behavior (T) which teaches the child to look for alternative behaviors when encountering future limitations.

The play therapist makes certain to use all three parts of the model.

A   Acknowledge the Feeling
C   Communicate the Limit
T   Target an Alternative Behavior/Activity

Child: The child quickly looks at the therapist and begins painting on the floor.

Therapist: A   You really want to paint the floor.

             C   The floor is not for painting.

             T   Paper is for painting on.

Individuals Practice in Dyads or Triads

4. Provide the individual, group, or class with an opportunity to practice this skill.

   If possible, divide into groups of three. One person role-plays a child, one person the play therapist, and one the observer. The observer writes each response the play therapist makes to the child.

Play Therapist Acknowledges Own Strengths and One Area for Growth

5. At the end of the two to three minute role-play, the play therapist states what he or she did effectively and what he or she would like to change.

Observer Reviews Each of the Play Therapist's Responses

6. The observer reads aloud each of the play therapist's therapeutic responses and gives the copy of the responses to the play therapist.

Person Who Role-Played Child Reacts

7. The person who role-played the child gives specific feedback to the play therapist indicating how the play therapist's responses impacted him or her.

Observer: Use the numbered lines to write therapeutic responses.

Play Therapist: Use the second line (under the numbered lines) to make changes to your therapeutic response (if needed).

1. (A) _____

   (C) _____

   (T) _____

Corrected Response

   (A) _____

   (C) _____

   (T) _____

2. (A) _____

   (C) _____

   (T) _____

Corrected Response

   (A) _____

   (C) _____

   (T) _____

3. (A) _____

   (C) _____

   (T) _____

Corrected Response

   (A) _____

   (C) _____

   (T) _____

CHAPTER 20

VIDEO REVIEW — IDENTIFYING AND IMPROVING THERAPEUTIC RESPONSES
Acknowledging Non-Verbal Actions

Videotape a play therapy or a practice play session with a child. Review the videotape and complete the following tasks.

1. Write down all of the responses that acknowledge non-verbal behavior.

2. If the response could be improved, write an alternate response.

Review

1. Keep the focus on the child. (i.e., "*You are* making that car drive fast"; instead of, "*that car* is going really fast.")

2. Avoid labeling items the child has not yet labeled. (i.e., "You're pushing *that* into the sand"; instead of, "you're pushing that *block* deep into the sand.")

3. Were the responses conversational and genuine? Were the responses that acknowledge non-verbal actions used too frequently or infrequently?

1. _____

1a. _____

2. _____

2a. _____

3. _____

3a. _____

4. _____

4a. _____

5. _____

5a. _____

6. _____

6a. _____

7. _____

7a. _____

8. _____

8a. _____

9. _____

9a. _____

10. _____

10a. _____

Discuss strengths and areas in need of improvement. For example, was the tone of voice conversational and genuine? Were the responses provided at an effective pace or were the responses too infrequent or frequent?

_____

_____

_____

_____

_____

_____

Video Review — Identifying And Improving Therapeutic Responses

Reflecting Content

Videotape a play therapy or a practice play session with a child. Review the videotape and complete the following tasks.

1. Write down all of the responses that reflect content.

2. If the response could be improved, write an alternate response.

Review

Paraphrase the content of the child's message so that the child is not being parroted.

1. _____

1a. _____

2. _____

2a. _____

3. _____

3a. _____

4. _____

4a. _____

5. _____

5a. _____

6. _____

6a. _____

7. _____

7a. _____

8. _____

8a. _____

9. _____

9a. _____

10. _____

10a. _____

Discuss strengths and areas in need of improvement. For example, was th to of voice conversational and genuine? Were the responses provided at an effective pace? Did the responses paraphrase or parrot the child's

_____

_____

_____

_____

_____

_____

Video Review — Identifying And Improving Therapeutic Responses

Reflecting Feeling

Videotape a play therapy or a practice play session with a child. Review the videotape and complete the following tasks.

    1. Write down all of the responses that reflect feeling.

    2. If the response could be improved, write an alternate response.

Review

    1. Keep the focus on the child. (i.e., You sound excited. You're angry that the toys aren't for throwing.)

    2. Identify the feeling as accurately as possible. Listen to the child's tone of voice and observe facial expressions and overall body language.

    3. Sometimes a play therapist may miss an opportunity to make a reflection of feeling. If this occurred, write the child's response and actions on the first line, and the reflection of feeling on the second line.

    4. Use the column on the far left to indicate whether or not the therapist's tone of voice was congruent with the child's affect. (Y = yes it was congruent with the child's affect or N = no it was not congruent with the child's affect.)

N / Y

_____   1. _____

_____   1a. _____

_____   2. _____

_____   2a. _____

_____   3. _____

_____   3a. _____

N/Y

_____   4. _____

_____   4a. _____

_____   5. _____

_____   5a. _____

_____   6. _____

_____   6a. _____

_____   7. _____

_____   7a. _____

_____   8. _____

_____   8a. _____

Discuss strengths and areas in need of improvement. For example, was the tone of voice conversational and genuine? When the child expressed feelings verbally or non-verbally, did the therapist acknowledge and reflect the child's feelings? Are any specific feelings (i.e., happiness, anger, sadness) difficult to identify or reflect?

_____

_____

_____

_____

_____

Video Review — Identifying And Improving Therapeutic Responses

Facilitating Esteem-Building And Encouragement

Videotape a play therapy or a practice play session with a child. Review the videotape and complete the following tasks.

1. Write down all of the responses that facilitate esteem-building and encouragement.

2. If the response could be improved, write an alternate response.

Review

1. A play therapist may "positively evaluate" a child (i.e., you're really smart). This type of response encourages the child to look outside himself and toward others for additional praise and approval. Instead, the therapist wants the child to learn to acknowledge the child's own attributes and efforts. Instead of telling a child, "you're really smart," the therapist responds "you know a lot about dinosaurs." The child is able to reflect on this statement and acknowledge this skill or ability in himself (i.e., I do know a lot about dinosaurs.)

2. Sometimes a play therapist may miss an opportunity to facilitate esteem-building or encouragement. For example, the therapist may praise the child (i.e., great job) instead of offering encouragement (i.e., you worked hard to make that painting.) If this occurred, write the response that "praised" the child on the first line and an esteem-building or encouraging response on the second line.

1. _____

1a. _____

2. _____

2a. _____

3. _____

3a. _____

4. _____

4a. _____

5. _____

5a. _____

6. _____

6a. _____

7. _____

7a. _____

8. _____

8a. _____

Discuss strengths and areas in need of improvement. What is the major difference between general praise (i.e., great job) and encouragement? How does general praise versus encouragement impact a child? Was it challenging to avoid general praise?

_____

_____

_____

_____

_____

_____

_____

Video Review — Identifying And Improving Therapeutic Responses

Facilitating Decision-Making And Responsibility

Videotape a play therapy or a practice play session with a child. Review the videotape and complete the following tasks.

1. Write down all of the responses that facilitate decision-making and responsibility.

2. If the response could be improved, write an alternate response.

Review

2. A child may look to others for help making decisions that the child is capable of making on her own. A child may ask for help when the child is capable of accomplishing a task on her own. It is important that the play therapist encourage the child to make a decision or accomplish a task without assistance. (i.e., It's up to you to decide what you'd like to do.)

3. Some children need opportunities to take initiative and develop a sense of responsibility. Responses such as "you decided to put on the cape" or "you have a plan" acknowledge the child's abilities to make decisions and take responsibility.

4. Sometimes a play therapist may miss an opportunity to facilitate decision-making or responsibility. For example, the therapist may answer a child's question (i.e., "should I play in the sandbox or with the dollhouse?" with a response such as "play with the dollhouse first.") This does not provide the child with the opportunity to take responsibility and make a decision. If this occurred, write the therapist's response that missed the opportunity to facilitate decision-making on the first line and a response that facilitates decision-making and responsibility on the second line.

1. _____

1a. _____

2. _____

2a. _____

3. _____

3a. _____

4. _____

4a. _____

5. _____

5a. _____

6. _____

6a. _____

7. _____

7a. _____

8. _____

8a. _____

Discuss strengths and areas in need of improvement.

_____

_____

_____

_____

_____

_____

Video Review — Identifying And Improving Therapeutic Responses

Limit-Setting — Using the ACT Model

Videotape a play therapy or a practice play session with a child. Review the videotape and complete the following tasks.

1. Write down all of the limit-setting responses.

2. If the response could be improved, write an alternate response.

Review

1. The therapist sets limits to protect the child, the therapist, the toys, and the room and to structure the session and limit socially unacceptable behavior.

2. Limits insure a safe and secure environment and teach self-control and self-responsibility. Limits need to be consistent and stated in a calm, patient, and firm voice.

3. Sometimes a play therapist may miss an opportunity to set a limit or the play therapist does not use the entire ACT model. If this occurred, write what happened (in the session/video) in the #1, 2, 3 and the corrected response using the ACT model in #1a, 2a, 3a.

1. A _____ message? ___

    C _____

    T _____

1a. A _____

    C _____

    T _____

2. A _____

    C _____

    T _____

2a. A _____

    C _____

    T _____

3. A _____

    C _____

    T _____

3a. A _____

    C _____

    T _____

Discuss strengths and areas in need of improvement. Was the therapist's tone of voice calm, patient, and firm?

_____

_____

_____

_____

_____

_____

Video Review — Identifying And Improving Therapeutic Responses

Videotape a play therapy or a practice play session with a child. Review the videotape and complete the following tasks.

1. Write down the first twenty-two therapeutic responses made by the play therapist.

2. Label the therapeutic response.

- AA   Acknowledging Non-Verbal Actions
- RC   Reflecting Content
- RF   Reflecting Feeling
- FEE   Facilitating Esteem-Building and Encouragement
- FDR   Facilitating Decision-Making and Responsibility
- LS   Limit-Setting

3. If the response could be improved, write an alternate response. For example, if the response acknowledged non-verbal actions and it could have reflected feeling or facilitated esteem-building write a different response. If the ACT model was used for limit-setting, but one part of it was eliminated from the response write an alternate response.

_____   1. _____

_____   1a. _____

_____   2. _____

_____   2a. _____

_____   3. _____

_____   3a. _____

_____   4. _____

_____   4a. _____

_____   5.   _____

_____   5a.   _____

_____   6.   _____

_____   6a.   _____

_____   7.   _____

_____   7a.   _____

_____   8.   _____

_____   8a.   _____

_____   9.   _____

_____   9a.   _____

_____   10.   _____

_____   10a.   _____

_____   11.   _____

_____   11a.   _____

_____   12.   _____

_____   12a.   _____

_____   13.   _____

_____   13a.   _____

_____   14. _____

_____   14a. _____

_____   15. _____

_____   15a. _____

_____   16. _____

_____   16a. _____

_____   17. _____

_____   17a. _____

_____   18. _____

_____   18a. _____

_____   19. _____

_____   19a. _____

_____   20. _____

_____   20a. _____

_____   21. _____

_____   21a. _____

_____   22. _____

_____   22a. _____

215

PLAY THERAPY VIDEO REVIEW

1. Briefly describe the child's verbal content or actions prior to the therapist's response.

2. Write therapist's response and label the therapeutic response.

- AA Acknowledging Non-Verbal Actions
- RC Reflecting Content
- RF Reflecting Feeling
- FEE Facilitating Esteem-Building and Encouragement
- FDR Facilitating Decision-Making and Responsibility
- LS Limit-Setting

3. Write an alternate or improved therapeutic response.

1a. _____

1b. _____

1c. _____

2a. _____

2b. _____

2c. _____

3a. _____

3b. _____

3c. _____

4a. _____

4b. _____

4c. _____

5a. _____

5b. _____

5c. _____

6a. _____

6b. _____

6c. _____

7a. _____

7b. _____

7c. _____

8a. _____

8b. _____

8c. _____

9a. _____

9b. _____

9c. _____

10a. _____

10b. _____

10c. _____

PLAY THERAPY VIDEO REVIEW

1. Briefly describe the child's verbal content or actions prior to the therapist's response.

2. Write therapist's response and label the therapeutic response.

- AA   Acknowledging Non-Verbal Actions
- RC   Reflecting Content
- RF   Reflecting Feeling
- FEE   Facilitating Esteem-Building and Encouragement
- FDR   Facilitating Decision-Making and Responsibility
- LS   Limit-Setting

3. Write an alternate or improved therapeutic response.

1a. _____

1b. _____

1c. _____

2a. _____

2b. _____

2c. _____

3a. _____

3b. _____

3c. _____

4a. _____

4b. _____

4c. _____

5a. _____

5b. _____

5c. _____

6a. _____

6b. _____

6c. _____

7a. _____

7b. _____

7c. _____

8a. _____

8b. _____

8c. _____

9a. _____

9b. _____

9c. _____

10a. _____

10b. _____

10c. _____

Questions for Supervision Meetings

General Questions for Use in Supervision

1. What did the therapist like about how she or he responded during the play therapy session?

2. What would the therapist like to change about how she or he responded during the play therapy session?

3. Supervisor: provide feedback on two positive qualities/characteristics. Provide one or two areas for growth.

Questions to Be Used While Reviewing the Play Therapy Session Videotape

1. What would you like have said to the child at this point?
2. What were you thinking at that time?
3. What thoughts were you having about what the child was doing?
4. What message do you think the child was trying to give you?
5. How do you think the child was feeling about you and the play therapy session?
6. Do you think the child was aware of your feelings or thoughts?
7. Do you think the child felt understood and listened to?

Encouraging the Child to Lead

What does the child learn from leading the process?

Quality of Non-Verbal Responses

1. Is the play therapist's body posture relaxed and comfortable?
2. Is there an absence of fidgeting?
3. Does the therapist look interested in the child?

Quality of Therapeutic Responses

1. What is important about keeping therapeutic responses short and succinct?

2. How could making too few therapeutic responses affect the child?

3. How could making too many therapeutic responses affect the child?

4. How can the play therapist make therapeutic responses interactive and conversational?

Congruence

1. Is the therapist's tone of voice congruent with the child's affect?

2. Is the therapist's facial expression congruent with the therapist's responses?

3. Is the therapist's tone of voice and expression congruent with the therapist's responses?

PLAY THERAPY ORGANIZATIONS

Association for Play Therapy
2050 N. Winery Avenue, Suite 101
Fresno, CA 93703
559-252-2278
www.a4pt.org

Play Therapy International
11E 900 Greenbank Road, Suite 527
Nepean (Ottawa), Ontario
Canada K2J 4P6
613-634-3125
www.playtherapy.org

The Center for Play Therapy
University of North Texas
P.O. Box 13857
Denton, TX 76203-6857
940-565-3864
www.coe.unt.edu/cdhe/cpt/index.htm

REFERENCES

Axline, V. (1947). *Play therapy: The inner dynamics of childhood.* Cambridge, MA: Houghton Mifflin.

Guerney, L. (1972). *A training manual for parents.* Mimeographed report.

Landreth, L. (2002). *Play therapy: The art of the relationship.* (2nd ed.). New York: Brunner Routledge.

Rogers, C. (1942). *Counseling and psychotherapy.* Boston: Houghton Mifflin.